PERFECT DAY
CALIFORNIA

Daily Itineraries for the Discerning Traveler

Christopher P. Baker

Reedy Press
PO Box 5131
St. Louis, MO 63139
www.reedypress.com

Library of Congress Control Number: 2021935155
ISBN: 9781681063300

Cover and interior design: Eric Marquard

Printed in the United States of America
21 22 23 24 25 5 4 3 2 1

Title page images *(clockwise from top left)*:
1. Catalina Island Hummer Tour. (Courtesy Catalina Island Company)
2. Hearst Castle. (Copyright Christopher P. Baker)
3. Birch Aquarium at Scripps, Child at Kelp Forest Tank. (Copyright & courtesy Joanne DiBona)
4. Railtown 1897 State Historic Park. (Credit Menka Belgal; courtesy Visit Tuolumne County)
5. Mission San Juan Capistrano basilica. (Copyright Roman Eugeniusz, CC BY-SA 3.0, via Wikimedia Commons)
6. Lick Observatory. (Courtesy San Jose CVB)
7. Calistoga, Old Faithful geyser. (Courtesy Visit Calistoga)
8. Golden Gate Bridge from Baker Beach. (Credit Billy Huynh; courtesy San Francisco Travel Authority)

Dedication

To the memory of my dear friend and
fellow travel journalist Lee Foster

PERFECT DAY
CALIFORNIA

Daily Itineraries for the Discerning Traveler

The waterfront and Golden Gate Bridge.
(Credit Umer Sayyam;
courtesy San Francisco Travel Authority)

Contents

Palm Springs Aerial Tramway. (Courtesy Palm Springs CVB)

Insets above *(left to right)*:
Laguna Beach Art Trail, Laguna Art Museum. (Courtesy Laguna Art Museum);
Petersen Automotive Museum, 'Seeing Red' exhibit. (Courtesy Petersen
Automotive Museum); Brophy Bros. seafood. (Courtesy Brophy Bros.)

Monterey Bay Aquarium, suspended orca. (Copyright Christopher P. Baker)

Drive North Lake Tahoe to Emerald Bay. (Courtesy Lake Tahoe Visitors Authority)

Insets above *(left to right)*: Queen Mary at sunset. (Courtesy Queen Mary); Ballooning in Sonoma. (Courtesy Sonoma Ballooning); Disneyland, Mickey Mouse. (Credit Joshua Sudock; courtesy Disneyland Resort)

Introduction

Nowhere else in the United States is as staggeringly diverse as California. Stretching 840 miles north-south and 365 miles at its widest, the "Golden State" is a region of breathtaking beauty—from the sun-kissed beaches of Southern California and mist-shrouded coast redwood forests of the north to the extremes of Death Valley, the grandeur of the snow-capped Sierra Nevada, and the lush vineyards of Sonoma and Napa. Then there's the urban excitement, spanning culturally rich San Diego, Los Angeles, and San Francisco to rustic yesteryear Gold Country enclaves.

There's something for everyone, from aquariums to zoos! Add in museums and a kaleidoscope of eclectic attractions, from Disneyland to the NASA Jet Propulsion Laboratory, and don't forget all the thrilling active adventures, such as bicycling and hot-air ballooning.

You could spend a lifetime exploring California. But what if have only one day in each destination? I've spent four decades exploring my home state tip to toe for vacations and as a professional travel journalist. Here, I've selected my favorite venues and activities that I believe comprise a "perfect day" for each of 29 top cities and destinations. And to break your day, I've selected some of my favorite restaurants. Enjoy!

Christopher P. Baker
Palm Springs, California

SAN DIEGO

SAN DIEGO—California's quintessential beach town, as well as its second largest and most southerly city— perfectly evokes the state's sun-drenched outdoor lifestyle. With its gorgeous Mediterranean climate, vast deep-water harbor, and fabulous beaches, the city is primed for hiking, biking, and surfing. Though it's tempting to spend your day soaking up the sun and the stunning setting, dedicate your precious time to the city's fascinating history and culture.

Founded in 1769, the city has plenty of historic draws. Get a feel for local life two centuries ago in Old Town San Diego. The Gaslamp Quarter will transport you back to the late 19th century, and the Maritime Museum of San Diego and USS *Midway* will immerse you in the city's long naval history. Above all, don't miss Balboa Park, boasting 17 world-class museums *plus* the incomparable and irresistibly endearing San Diego Zoo—and we're just getting started!

San Diego Zoo

2920 Zoo Drive • 619-231-1515
sandiegozoowildlifealliance.org

☑ From oh-so-cute polar bears staring at you through an underwater glass wall to a chance to hand-feed an endangered rhino, the cool experiences here are indelible. They're also two of the reasons San Diego Zoo is considered the world's finest zoo.

Spanning 100 acres in the northwest corner of Balboa Park, this glee-inducing venue displays more than 4,000 animals representing 800-plus species—from binturongs to Tasmanian devils—in enclosures resembling their natural habitats.

Nine animal zones represent distinct geographical areas. Don't miss **Lost Forest**, a lush African rainforest roamed by Western lowland gorillas; the walk-through **Scripps Aviary**, where more than 130 African birds fly free overhead; **Tiger Trail**, where striped Malaysian tigers prowl a mock equatorial jungle; and **Polar Bear Plunge**, where three Arctic bruins frolic in a 130,000-gallon pool and, on special-treat days, even in snow!

To get the lay of the park, first hop on the open-air, double-decker bus for a 35-minute guided tour. And a worth-the-splurge Inside Look Tours and VIP Experience will get you even more up-close and personal with the animals.

San Diego Zoo, Polar Bear Plunge.
(Credit Christina Simmons; courtesy San Diego Zoo Wildlife Alliance)

Balboa Park, Automotive Museum. (Copyright and courtesy Joanne DiBona)

Balboa Park

1549 El Prado • 619-239-0512
www.balboapark.org

Immediately south of the zoo, this vast cultural oasis is the largest of its kind in the United States. Created in 1868, the landscaped 1,200-acre green swathe was graced with Spanish Colonial pavilions built for the 1915 Panama-California Exposition. Today, its iconic vernacular buildings house 17 museums and cultural venues linked by traffic-free promenades. Pick up a map and audio tour at the visitor center on El Prado, and plan a route taking in your desired sites.

Start at the **Natural History Museum**, focusing on evolution from the dinosaur era to the current day. Next, head to the **Reuben H. Fleet Science Center**, with fascinating interactive science exhibits. Now make a beeline for the world-class **Museum of Art**, spanning collections from European masters to contemporary Californian maestros. Nearby, the **Museum of Us** has enthralling exhibits on human anthropology. And in Pan American Plaza, the **Automotive Museum** boasts a fabulous assemblage of rare historic autos and motorcycles, while the **Air & Space Museum** wows visitors with a superb collection that even includes the Apollo IX Command Module spacecraft.

Bare Back Grill

4640 Mission Boulevard • 858-274-7117
www.barebackgrill.com

☑ Laid-back in true San Diego surfer fashion, this fun, casual California grill is just steps from the beach in the Pacific Beach neighborhood. The Kiwi owners—avid surfers—play up the unpretentious "down under" feel with a wood-heavy New Zealand motif that enhances the restaurant's cool coastal vibe. Aside from the surfboards adorning the wall and wooden ceiling, the decor is low key. Like any good sports bar, it has flat-screen TVs and an ever-changing selection of craft beers.

Trust the locals, who swear by the artisanal burgers, consistently voted best in San Diego for good reason. The growler specials are made of hormone-free, grass-fed organic beef and lamb from New Zealand. Served with sides of sweet potato fries and wasabi dip, they're cooked to perfection. The Kiwilango Burger, laden with blue cheese crumbles, lettuce, tomato, red onion, and fresh diced jalapeños, oozes a dozen mouthwatering flavors. Chalkboards list daily specials, including such breakfasts as house crab cakes with poached eggs and spinach, tempura fried calamari with sweet peppers for lunch, and fish 'n' chips and chicken pot pie to round off the evening.

Bareback Grill.
(Courtesy Bareback Grill)

Nearby Alternatives
Outdoors: Gaslamp Quarter

For better or worse, the notorious bars, brothels, and gambling dens of San Diego's boom years in the late 19th century are gone. But this National Historic District delights with its 16 blocks of renovated grand Victorian buildings and gas lamps. It teems at night as the city's lively cultural heart.
614 Fifth Avenue
619-233-5227
www.gaslamp.org

Viewpoint: Cabrillo National Monument

You can't beat the views at the windswept tip of Point Loma, where on September 28, 1542, Spanish conquistador Juan Rodríguez Cabrillo became the first European to set foot on what is now California. The visitor center is a superb museum, and you can peruse the Old Point Loma Lighthouse.
1800 Cabrillo Memorial Drive
619-523-4285
www.nps.gov/cabr/index.htm

Museum: Maritime Museum of San Diego

The Maritime Museum boasts a world-class collection of historic ships. Board the *Star of India* four-masted barque built in 1863. Squeeze inside the Soviet B-39 and USS *Dolphin* submarines. Then walk south to the USS *Midway* Museum (*www.midway.org*) to explore this decommissioned aircraft carrier with 30 restored aircraft on display.
1492 North Harbor Drive
619-234-9153, ext. 101
www.sdmaritime.org

Museum and Restaurant: Old Town San Diego State Historic Park

For a glimpse of the lifestyles two centuries ago, head to this historic park featuring more than 20 original buildings established by the Spanish beginning in 1821 near the San Diego River. Today housing museums, restaurants, and shops that recapture the energy of the erstwhile settlement, it's a fascinating and fun-filled visit.
2415 San Diego Avenue
619-291-4903
www.parks.ca.gov/?page_id=663

Trip Planning
San Diego Visitor Information Center

996-B North Harbor Drive
619-737-2999
www.sandiegovisit.org

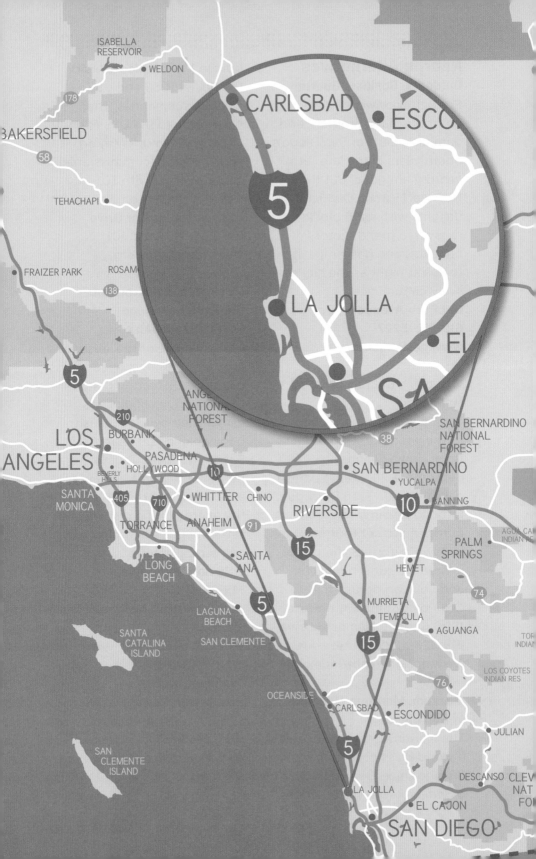

LA JOLLA

ONLY MINUTES NORTH from downtown San Diego, this serene seaside suburb spans seven miles of curvaceous coastline that will leave you agog at its beauty. From its picturesque Mediterranean village-like setting above crashing waves to stellar attractions and casual cosmopolitan luxury lifestyle, La Jolla—pronounced "La Hoya"—promises a sun-kissed Southern California experience like no other.

Add to that gorgeous beaches, coves with tide pools, dramatic ocean bluffs, a stellar art museum, not to mention a world-class aquarium, unique coastal ecological reserve, and underwater marine reserve! Then there's downtown—the Village—with its art galleries, designer clothes shops, gourmet chocolatiers, and chic restaurants. No wonder La Jolla is a favorite of Hollywood stars, many of whose fab hillside homes afford some of the most sublime coastal vistas in California. While you may not be able to afford to live here, this perfect 24-hour itinerary guarantees a brief taste of the good life.

La Jolla Coast Walk Trail

Coast Walk and Torrey Pines Road
www.lajollabythesea.com/listings/la-jolla-walking-trail

The quintessential La Jolla experience is surely to walk the scenic cliff-top trail that begins at Coast Walk and Torrey Pines Road (park on Prospect Place) and snakes along the waterfront to **Seal Rock**. Laid out in 1932, it unspools for two miles—an easy stroll with, on your left, quaint cottages and gorgeous mansions edging right up to the azure ocean on your right.

At **Goldfish Point** overlook, peer down into the clear jade-colored waters of La Jolla Underwater Ecological Reserve and look for orange Garibaldis, the California state marine fish. The cove on the south side features La Jolla Caves; from **The Cave Store**, you can follow 144 steps down an old bootlegger's tunnel to **Sunny Jim Cave**.

Further along, La Jolla Cove has a beach and is the perfect spot for snorkeling and swimming. Beyond, at **Point La Jolla**, the trail turns south past **Shell Beach**, cusping flat-topped **Seal Rock**—a fave hot spot for harbor seals to bask in the sun. End your walk immediately south at the **Children's Pool**, a lovely secluded beach.

La Jolla Walk Trail. (Courtesy Georges at the Cove)

Museum of Contemporary Art, 'Pleasure Point'.
(Courtesy Museum of Contemporary Art San Diego)

Museum of Contemporary Art (MOCA)

700 Prospect Street
858-454-3541 • www.mcasd.org

✓ Andy Warhol, Roy Lichtenstein, Robert Irwin, and an A-list of Latin American artists—what's not to love about this fabulous museum displaying constantly rotating exhibits from its permanent collection of 4,700-plus post-1950 artworks? In 2021, this companion of the Museum of Contemporary Art San Diego emerged from a far-reaching expansion and remake that exploits its prime oceanfront location in the Village with two levels of light-filled galleries, soaring ceilings, and vast vertical windows offering sensational vistas.

Thrill to a colorful palette of Pop Art, including Warhol's *Campbell's Soup Cans* (1962) and *Liz Taylor Diptych* (1963). Puzzle over Robert Irwin's modernist conceptual pieces, such as *Who's Afraid of Red, Yellow and Blue* (2006), which fills an entire room. Then, admire the more traditional *Housekeeper Series* portraits of maids with deadpan stares or shy smiles by Mexican artist Alida Cervantes. And don't miss the outside **Edwards Sculpture Garden** and MOCA's pièce de résistance, Nancy Rubins's *Pleasure Point* (2006)—a jumble of real-life surfboards, kayaks, Jet Skis, and rowboats cantilevered above the oceanfront terrace and kept afloat by high-tension wires.

George's at the Cove

1250 Prospect Street • 858-454-4244 • www.georgesatthecove.com

☑ A minimalist triptych that's cool, classy, contemporary, and oh-so SoCal, George's at the Cove offers a choice of distinct restaurants and bars on three levels with stunning views over the Pacific Ocean. Long a trendy staple of La Jolla, it's *the* place to enjoy award-winning cuisine and the La Jolla lifestyle.

California Modern, on the lower level, is home to Chef Trey Foshee's signature gourmet restaurant and bar. This chic farm-to-table fine-dining mecca serves inventive California fusion fare crafted from locally grown seasonal ingredients. Its emphasis is on tasting menus that celebrate the flavors of San Diego.

The popular rooftop Ocean Terrace—best enjoyed at sunset—offers a casual California Bistro menu and million-dollar ocean views alfresco year-round. Its exciting menu spans fresh fish tacos to such mouthwatering treats as mussels with lemongrass, coconut milk, lime, ginger, beech mushrooms, cilantro, basil, and chili oil.

Sandwiched between California Modern and Ocean Terrace, George's Level2 is cocktail central. Stick to the classics or try such house creations as the signature Sea3 margarita with seaweed-laced ice cubes.

Georges at the Cove. (Courtesy Georges at the Cove)

Nearby Alternatives

Restaurant: The Cottage

Start the day with eggs Benedict or granola with fruit and yogurt at this quaint cottage restaurant. With its shaded patio dining behind a white picket fence, locals consider it tops for breakfast or brunch. It serves classic American faves, from brioche French toast and lemon-ricotta pancakes to salmon hash and meatloaf.

7702 Fay Avenue
858-454-8409
www.cottagelajolla.com

Museum: Birch Aquarium at Scripps Institute of Oceanography

Explore the wonders of the Pacific Ocean and be amazed by the sea creatures at this spectacular aquarium. Its state-of-the-art exhibits span distinct marine habitats, from **Hall of Fishes** and **Seadragons & Seahorses** to the sunlit giant kelp forest tank with wave-making machine. Youngsters will enjoy the sea-life touch pools!

2300 Expedition Way
858-534-3474
www.aquarium.ucsd.edu

Outdoors: Torrey Pines State Reserve

Hikers and nature lovers can explore miles of trails in this 2,000-acre coastal wilderness of eerily eroded seaside cliffs and copses of wind-sculpted pines—*Pinus torreyana*—endemic to the reserve. On the park's north edge, **Los Peñasquitos Marsh** draws migrating seabirds and waterfowl. The visitor center offers guided nature walks.

12600 North Torrey Pines Road
858-755-2063
www.parks.ca.gov/?page_id=657

Outdoors: La Jolla Tide Pools

Kids especially will love tide-pooling in the cliffside tide pools along seven miles of La Jolla coastline. Easily accessible, these pools teem with creatures from anemones and crabs to octopi and sea stars. Be sure to visit at low tide, and, remember, the pools are marine protected environments, so removing marine life is illegal. Birch Aquarium offers Tidepooling Adventures.

www.aquarium.ucsd.edu/conservation/our-work/tidepools

Trip Planning

La Jolla Village Merchants Association
7590 Fay Avenue, Suite 404
858-230-2725
www.lajollabythesea.com

LAGUNA BEACH

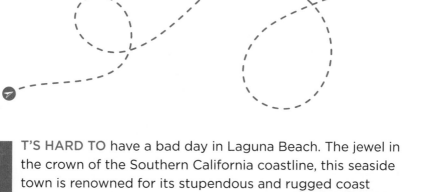

I'S HARD TO have a bad day in Laguna Beach. The jewel in the crown of the Southern California coastline, this seaside town is renowned for its stupendous and rugged coast scenery and hip and artsy Mediterranean-like lifestyle. In fact, Laguna first evolved as an artist colony. Today, there are myriad ways to enjoy the art here, starting, of course, at the Laguna Art Museum, followed by a leisurely self-guided public art tour through Heisler Park and the galleries lining Pacific Highway. The highway unfurls south to nearby San Juan Capistrano, with a superb historic mission to explore that makes for a tremendous half-day excursion.

Toss in options for fabulous tide-pooling in the coves and beaches, hiking the Crystal Cove State Park wilderness mere steps from the sands, or having close-up educational encounters with sea lions and seals at the Pacific Marine Mammal Center, and you have the combination for a perfect day in Laguna Beach.

Laguna Beach Art Tour

Laguna Beach Visitor Center • 381 Forest Avenue • 949-497-9229 or
800-877-1115 • www.visitlagunabeach.com • www.lagunabeachwalks.com
www.lagunabeacharttours.com

✓ As famous for its artsy culture as for its coves and beaches,
Laguna Beach is truly an art-lover's haven. It's lined with
art galleries, studded with public art pieces, and boasts a stellar
art museum (plus one of the foremost art festivals in the United
States—the Pageant of the Masters—where famous works of art
are brought to life onstage nightly, June–September). A half-day
walking tour is a must, yet it's barely enough!

Start at the **Laguna Art Museum** (*www.lagunaartmuseum.org*)—
a trove of modern and contemporary works by California artists.
North Coast Highway just north of the museum is nicknamed
"Gallery Row," with dozens of galleries to browse. The galleries
host an Art Walk on the first Thursday of each month. One block
west, oceanside **Heitzler Park** teems with many of the city's more
than 100 public art pieces. Don't miss Jon Seeman's 16-foot-tall
sculpture, *Breaching Whale* (2011), and Terry Thornsley's mural
Grace (2014) honoring Laguna Beach lifeguards. The *Laguna
Beach Public Art Collection* online booklet is a handy pocket guide
to tote along and help you plan your own route.

Laguna Beach Art Trail, Laguna Art Museum. (Courtesy Laguna Art Museum)

Mission San Juan Capistrano basilica.
(Copyright Roman Eugeniusz, CC BY-SA 3.0, via Wikimedia Commons)

Mission San Juan Capistrano

26801 Ortega Highway • 949-234-1300 • www.missionsjc.com

✓ Nicknamed the "Jewel of the Missions" for its architectural beauty, Mission San Juan Capistrano makes for a memorable visit, especially in early spring when swallows famously return from Argentina each year to nest. Yes, they are the ones immortalized in the Ink Spot's song "When the Swallows Come Back to Capistrano."

Founded in 1776 as the seventh of the 21 California missions, it suffered greatly due to natural disasters. Entering the grounds, on your right is the ruin of the original church (the largest in the mission chain), toppled by an earthquake in 1812. The **Bell Wall** survived, however, and still contains its four bells above a life-size statue of founder Father Junípero Serra. The **Serra Chapel**, with its stunning gilt altar, has been restored to former glory.

A fascinating audio tour is provided with admission to give you a complete understanding of mission life and layout as you roam the various museum rooms with their excellent interpretive displays. Or you can take a twice-daily guided tour. Next, walk north 200 yards to admire the **Mission Basilica**.

Nick's

440 South Coast Highway • 949-376-8595
www.nicksrestaurants.com

✓ You may have to wait to get into this uber-popular, heart-of-downtown, first-come-first-served restaurant and Southern California institution (it also has outlets in Long Beach, Manhattan Beach, Pasadena, and San Clemente), but it's a wait richly repaid. With luck, you'll snap up a place on the raised roadside patio—perfect for people-watching and even a view of the beach. But inside is cool, too, with its exposed brick walls, cozy booths, and a central island bar beneath a skylit atrium.

Carnivores swear that Nick's makes the best prime rib sandwich of all time, which highlights a menu of classic American dishes such as succulent cheeseburgers, awesome rib eye melts, buttermilk fried chicken, and even San Francisco cioppino. The kitchen also puts out mean salads, sandwiches, and a daily-rotating soup menu, plus the restaurant's signature fried asparagus spears. Or try the spicy Filet Mignon Chili—another signature dish—with skillet-baked corn bread, best combined with a jalapeño-watermelon margarita house cocktail, perhaps. If the wait to be seated is too long, Nick's also offers a selection of takeout dishes.

Nick's, market salad.
(Courtesy Nick's
Restaurant)

Nearby Alternatives

Educational Venue: Ocean Institute

On weekends, Dana Point's Ocean Institute is a great place for adults and kids to enjoy engaging enrichment experiences that teach about California's maritime history and the Pacific's marine environment. Along with touch tanks, you can even take kayak tours or sail aboard the *Spirit of Dana Point* schooner.
24200 Dana Point Harbor Drive, Dana Point
949-496-2274
www.oceaninstitute.org

Outdoors: Crystal Cove State Park

Extending inland from Crystal Cove up thickly wooded Moro Canyon, this undeveloped wilderness boasts more than three miles of pristine beach, fabulous tide pools, and rugged and hilly backcountry laced with trails. Check out the website for tidal pool walks, guided hikes, geology talks, and other interpretive programs by park docents.
8471 North Coast Highway
949-494-3539
www.crystalcovestatepark.org

Educational Venue: Pacific Marine Mammal Center

Children especially adore visiting this marine rescue center, where California sea lions and occasionally northern elephant seals, northern fur seals, and Pacific harbor seals found stranded or injured are nursed back to health for release back to the wild. Plus, you can wander the center's Butterfly Garden. Entrance is free.
20612 Laguna Canyon Road
949-494-3050
www.pacificmmc.org

Outdoors: Laguna Beach Tide Pools

Laguna Beach is renowned for its sensational tide pools—a marine protected area. So, spend half a day exploring for anemones, hermit crabs, sea stars, and more at any of about a dozen stellar beaches and coves, from the easily accessible rock shelf at Main Beach and Crescent Bay Beach to the deep, secluded pools at Thousand Steps.
www.visitlagunabeach.com

Trip Planning

Laguna Beach Visitor Center
381 Forest Avenue
949-497-9229 or 800-877-1115
www.visitlagunabeach.com

LONG BEACH

AT THE CENTER of the vast conurbation of Greater Los Angeles, Long Beach long struggled to profile its Cinderella appeal. Hugging an eight-mile, sand-fringed swathe of the Pacific Ocean, California's port city par excellence today wears a glass slipper after a decade of exciting revitalization.

Anchoring both the waterfront and a long list of landmark attractions is the *Queen Mary*, the retired yet still stately 1930s ocean liner. Alternatively, you can explore the Earl Burns Miller Japanese Garden, watch sea lions cavort at the Aquarium of the Pacific, or maybe spot dolphins and whales at play on the ocean passage to Catalina Island.

Culture vultures are in their element too. From the Long Beach Museum of Art (housed in a historic craftsman mansion) and the East Village Arts District (with its Museum of Latin American Art) to the waterside Long Beach Performing Arts Center, California's sixth-largest city is a center for world-class arts.

Aquarium of the Pacific

100 Aquarium Way · 562-590-3100 · www.aquariumofpacific.org

✓ Did you know that 10 out of the world's 17 penguin species live in temperate zones and never see ice or snow? Did you even realize they're birds, with thick, heavy bones and wings like flippers allowing them to dive and "fly" underwater? A metaphorical journey of discovery through the world's largest ocean, the Aquarium of the Pacific offers a fascinating insight into Magellanic Penguins and more than 500 other marine species in exhibits spanning the frigid waters of Antarctica to the colorful reefs of the Tropical Pacific.

The vast outdoor **Shark Lagoon** is worth the visit alone with its 150-plus sharks, some of which you can touch. . . *and some you can't!* There's also a sea jelly touch tank. Hands-on behind-the-scenes tours let you interact with seals, sea lions, sea otters, and even giant octopi. And you can purchase a cup of nectar to feed the birds as you walk through the **Lorikeet Forest** aviary. The aquarium even offers daily whale watch cruises. Next, hop aboard the **AquaBus** water taxi to the *Queen Mary*.

Aquarium of the Pacific, Long Beach. (Credit Sean Arbabi; courtesy Visit California)

Queen Mary at sunset. (Courtesy *Queen Mary*)

Queen Mary

1126 Queens Highway • 562-435-3510
www.queenmary.com

✓ The jewel in the crown of the Cunard White Star Line when launched in 1936, the *Queen Mary* was the world's most luxurious and technologically advanced ocean liner. She made 1,001 weekly transatlantic crossings from Southampton to New York City before retiring in 1967, when she was purchased by the City of Long Beach and permanently docked for use as a hotel and tourist attraction. Now listed on the National Register of Historic Places and one of the Historic Hotels of America, she wows visitors with her restored art deco glory.

Revel in an exciting and informative guided tour as you explore the ship from bow to stern—maybe even down into the engine rooms on the **Steam and Steel Tour**—or thrill to a nonscary hunt for legendary ghosts on the **Haunted Encounters Tour**. You'll be fascinated by exhibitions such as the *Queen Mary's* duty as a troopship during World War II. And the original rich wood paneling and period decor will leave you agog! Don't be surprised if you find yourself wanting to stay overnight in one of 347 spacious staterooms.

Lola's Mexican Cuisine

2030 East Fourth Street • 562-343-5506 • www.lolasmexicancuisine.com

✓ Always humming, Lola's Mexican Cuisine is one of the busiest restaurants on Retro Row. Facing the classic art deco Art cinema, this family-run, vegan-friendly delight induces a kind of "have I stumbled into a Pixar animated movie?" feel with its fun *Dia de Los Muertos* (Day of the Dead) decor, including a smiling neon-lit skull on the façade. It has sidewalk seating and a lovely outdoor patio out back.

The owners pride themselves on serving recipes that Lola Navarro's *abuela* (grandma) passed down from when she was just a little girl growing up in Guadalajara, Mexico. Chef Luis Navarro has added to the menu by traveling throughout Mexico, learning regional specialties to create a blend of traditional and new contemporary dishes. They ensure things get off to a good start by serving yummy de rigueur chips and salsa. Everything is farm-to-table fresh, such as Tinga Tostaditas (pulled chicken simmered with chipotle and sweet onions over a spicy black bean pureé) and Jalisco Tacos, smothered with grilled corn, salsa, and sour cream and served with garlicky whole beans, fresh guacamole, and caramelized plantains.

Lola's Mexican Cuisine. (Courtesy Lola's Mexican Cuisine)

Nearby Alternatives

Museum: Long Beach Museum of Art

This small jewel hosts changing exhibitions of American decorative arts, early 20th-century European art, and California modernism and contemporary art. The gem is made complete by its setting: the 1912 craftsman-style Elizabeth Milbank Anderson House, magnificently perched atop an ocean bluff. Don't miss Claire Falkenstein's *Structure and Flow* water sculpture.

2300 East Coast Boulevard
562-439-2119
www.lbma.org

Museum: Museum of Latin American Art [MOLAA]

You may never have heard of most artists represented at MOLAA (the only museum in the United States dedicated to modern and contemporary Latin American art), but their stunning and visceral works will surely impress you. The Long Gallery features a work by an artist from every Latin American country.

628 Alamitos Avenue
562-437-1689 • www.molaa.org

Outdoors: Catalina Island

Make this a fun-filled full day! Hop aboard a Catalina Express (*www.catalinaexpress.com*) ferry or take a helicopter for the thrilling 22-mile ride to the largest of California's Channel Islands. Stroll picturesque Avalon, then explore the crystal-clear waters on an **Undersea Sub Expedition**, and search for bison in the island's rugged interior.

150 Metropole Avenue, Avalon
877-778-8322
www.visitcatalinaisland.com

Venue: Earl Burns Miller Japanese Garden

An intimate place of perfection, this impeccable 1.3-acre Japanese Garden, on the campus of California State University, Long Beach, is totally zen! Beyond the tile-roofed entrance gate, you'll discover an oasis of meditating calm as winding paths lead past waterfalls, a koi pond, and a three-tiered pagoda set amid a lush landscape that changes color with each season.

1250 Bellflower Boulevard
562-985-4111
www.csulb.edu/japanese-garden

Trip Planning

Long Beach Convention & Visitors Bureau

302 East Ocean Boulevard, Suite 1900
562-436-3645
www.visitlongbeach.com

LOS ANGELES

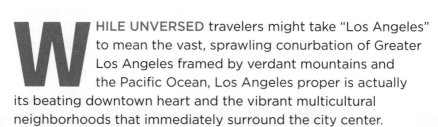

WHILE UNVERSED travelers might take "Los Angeles" to mean the vast, sprawling conurbation of Greater Los Angeles framed by verdant mountains and the Pacific Ocean, Los Angeles proper is actually its beating downtown heart and the vibrant multicultural neighborhoods that immediately surround the city center.

Downtown LA is packed with renowned museums, extraordinary performance and world-class art venues, and other dazzling highlights to thrill, inspire, and entertain even the most demanding of visitors. While glittering skyscrapers and urban hustle define LA in the popular imagination, the city core has plenty of hidden green spaces and ethnic enclaves, including distinctly Mexican El Pueblo de Los Angeles, Chinatown, Little Tokyo, and other little patches of traditional culture stitched on to the great quilt of this progressive city. With trailblazing restaurants, breathtaking rooftop bars, and an eclectic nightlife on top, there's no doubt that downtown LA is where the action is!

Downtown Walk

Historic Downtown Walking Tour, Saturdays at 10 a.m., $15
523 W. Sixth Street, Suite 826 • 213-623-2489 • www.laconservancy.org

✓ Downtown LA appears from afar as a sea of office towers such as architect I. M. Pei's 73-story First Interstate World Center (at 1,017 feet, the city's tallest building). But enough remains from the past that a walk through its palm-studded heart guarantees a new appreciation for the city.

Focus on the Greater Broadway area, starting at the **Bradbury Building** (*304 South Broadway*). This unassuming five-story Victorian-era office building, built in 1893, is renowned for its extraordinary ornamental iron atrium, famously featured in *Blade Runner*. Across Broadway, admire the baroque fantasy façade of the **Million Dollar Theater**. Immediately south, the **Grand Central Market** begs exploration. Exit the far side onto South Hill Street, where the 1901-era **Angels Flight Railway** funicular will carry you up Bunker Hill to **California Plaza**.

Walk one block north for the **Museum of Contemporary Art** (*www.moca.org*) to admire its stunning collection of postwar art by such luminaries as David Hockney, Roy Lichtenstein, and Mark Rothko. Allow one to two hours here, being sure to view Barbara Kruger's famous outdoor untitled mural. On MOCA's north side is the astonishing Frank Gehry-designed **Walt Disney Concert Hall**.

Downtown Los Angeles walk, Angels Flight funicular.
(Courtesy Los Angeles Tourism & Convention Board)

Exposition Park, *Endeavour* in California Science Center.
(Courtesy California Science Center)

Exposition Park

700 Exposition Park Drive • 213-744-2294 • www.expositionpark.ca.gov

✔ At the southwest corner of downtown, the quadrangular cluster of buildings and greens comprising Exposition Park was laid out in 1872 for agricultural fairs prior to becoming a public park. At its heart is the **LA Memorial Coliseum stadium**. The park's main attractions are on its north side surrounding the huge **Rose Garden**, planted in 1913.

Kids especially will thrill to the **Natural History Museum of Los Angeles County** (*www.nhm.org*). Boasting more than 35 million specimens, this stellar venue is outranked only by the Smithsonian, in Washington, DC. Not-to-miss ancient critters include the Dueling Dinosaurs exhibit in the foyer in which skeletons of a *triceratops* and *T. rex* battle it out . . . a prelude to an entire menagerie in Dinosaur Hall. The Schreiber Hall of Birds exhibits specimens from around the globe. The Gem and Mineral Hall literally sparkles. Local development is traced from the earliest humanoids in the Becoming Los Angeles exhibit.

Steps away, the **California Science Center** (*www.californiasciencecenter.org*) turns scientific and technological discovery into spellbinding fun with its interactive exhibits. The Air and Space Gallery—in a 1984 Frank Gehry structure—is a popular highlight; its fascinating displays include the space shuttle *Endeavour*. Or perhaps you'd prefer the adjoining **California African American Museum** (*www.caamuseum.org*), honoring the contribution of African Americans to American culture.

Bavel

500 Mateo Street • 213-232-4966
www.baveldtla.com

 One of Los Angeles's most exciting eateries, Bavel is a Middle Eastern restaurant in the Downtown Arts District. Opened in 2018, it became an instant hit as a sibling to Ori Menashe and Genevieve Gergis's other mega-hit restaurant: Bestia. Housed in an airy old warehouse sunlit through floor-to-ceiling windows, this laid-back space is enhanced by greenery hanging down from the soaring ceiling (it also has an outdoor patio).

Although you'll salivate over all the traditional Middle Eastern ingredients and dishes, there's nothing old-world about Menashe and Gergis's culinary approach. Both were born in the Los Angeles area, but their family roots span Egypt, Israel, Morocco, and Turkey. The couple showcase the cuisines of their family lineages. This being LA, they add a twist of modernity, of course, but without trying to totally reinvent baba ghanoush and other classics. For example, in addition to traditional—and deliciously creamy—hummus, you can savor a garlicky *hummus masabacha* with Yemeni *zhoug* hot sauce. Leave room for Genevieve's yummy desserts, such as rose clove chocolate donuts.

Bavel. (Courtesy Bavel)

Nearby Alternatives

Outdoors: Chinatown

Chinatown evolved in the 1870s immediately north of El Pueblo de Los Angeles and has gradually expanded northward. Check out the dim sung pagoda palaces and architecturally intriguing sites sandwiched between Hill and Broadway, with **Chinatown Central Plaza**—including its Bruce Lee statue and Gate of Filial Piety—its epicenter.
213-680-0243
943 North Broadway
www.chinatownla.com

Venue: El Pueblo de Los Angeles

The remains of a historic Spanish pueblo, the oldest part of the city is a State Historic Monument ablaze with color and mariachi music, especially during such festivals as Cinco de Mayo. Must-visits include the **Ávila Adobe** and **Old Plaza Church** (both built in 1818), and **Plaza de Cultura y Artes** (*www.lapca.org*).
125 Paseo de la Plaza
213-485-6855
elpueblo.lacity.org

Museum: Geffen Contemporary

Opened in 1983 as part of the MOCA complex, this spartan art space in the Little Tokyo Historic District occupies a former police garage redesigned by renowned architect Frank Gehry. Roam its 40,000 square feet of space dedicated to exhibitions by mostly young and emerging artists, including an experimental live-performance space.
152 North Central Avenue
213-626-6222
www.moca.org/visit/geffen-contemporary

Venue: Walt Disney Concert Hall

Home of the Los Angeles Philharmonic, this stupendous architectural masterpiece is instantly recognizable as a Frank Gehry design with its soaring, curvaceous stainless-steel panels. The hardwood-paneled main auditorium echoes the billowing sails theme. Take a self-guided audio tour, or book a guided tour. Be sure to visit the museum's **Blue Ribbon Garden**.
111 South Grand Avenue
323-850-2000
www.laphil.com

Trip Planning

Los Angeles Visitor Information Center, Union Station
800 North Alameda Street
213-239-1118
www.discoverlosangeles.com

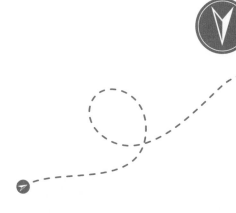

SANTA MONICA

FOUNDED IN THE 1890s and perched atop a plateau overlooking Santa Monica Bay, Santa Monica has ever since been considered *the* quintessential Los Angeles beach town, an acclaim boosted by the popular *Baywatch* TV series, filmed at Will Rogers State Beach. Evoked by detective-fiction writer (and Santa Monica resident) Raymond Chandler as "Bay City," it offers a perfect blend of endless sandy beaches, great surf, cool museums, an engaging arts scene, and some of the best cafés and restaurants in the LA basin.

Palm-shaded Palisades Park runs for 1.5 miles along the cliff top and offers spectacular views: on a clear day, you can even catch a view of Catalina Island, 22 miles away. Below, Santa Monica Pier, probing the Pacific, will prove an irresistible lure for a stroll. And the Santa Monica Mountains tempt hikers as well as culture vultures, who flock to the Getty Center and its incomparable J. Paul Getty Museum. Fantastic!

Santa Monica Pier

Ocean Avenue & Colorado Avenue • 310-458-8901 • www.santamonicapier.org

☑ Visiting Santa Monica without walking Santa Monica Pier—the West Coast's oldest pier—would be like visiting Paris without ascending the Eiffel Tower. The city's landmark pier extends 1,600 feet into the inviting waters of the Pacific Ocean, and it's packed with family-friendly attractions. It was built of concrete in 1909 as an excuse to run a sewage pipe beneath it out to sea (fortunately, the practice ended in the 1920s). The wider, shorter Promenade Pier, featuring almost all the attractions, was added alongside in 1916.

Take the air on the upper-deck **Pacific Park** (*www.pacpark.com*) boardwalk, lined with amusement arcades. Near the entrance is a venerable merry-go-round with 44 handcrafted ponies, plus the **Santa Monica Pier Aquarium**, with thrilling touch tanks full of local sea critters. At its west end, thrill to a roller coast, plus bumper cars, and a Ferris wheel rising 11 stories high. You can cast a line from designated fishing areas too.

Santa Monica Pier. (Courtesy Los Angeles Tourism & Convention Board)

Roman Sculpture Gallery at Getty Villa.
(Credit Sarah Waldorf; courtesy and copyright J. Paul Getty Trust)

Getty Center

1200 Getty Center Drive • 310-440-7300 • www.getty.edu/museum

☑ Poised proudly on a bluff of the Santa Monica Mountains, three miles northeast of Santa Monica, the $1 billion Getty Center enjoys a cultural stature equal to its commanding physical presence. Dominating the complex, its **J. Paul Getty Museum** displays the astonishing art collection of the eccentric eponymous oil tycoon.

Displayed in four skylit pavilions, the collection of more than 400 notable European paintings predating 1900 reveals Getty's predilection for Italian Renaissance and 17th-century Dutch and Flemish art. Begin in the **North Pavilion**, highlighting art from before 1600: don't miss Titian's *Portrait of Alfonso d'Avalos*, considered the Getty's most important portrait. The **East Pavilion** focuses on 17th- and 18th-century Dutch and Flemish painters, including Rembrandt and Rubens. Lovers of impressionism will delight in the **West Pavilion**, with its works by Cézanne, Manet, Monet, Renoir, Van Gogh (look for his famous *Irises*), and more. The **South Pavilion** is dedicated to decorative arts. Plus, there are photography exhibits, manuscripts, and a sculpture park.

The vast antiquities collection is on view at the **Getty Villa** (*17985 Pacific Coast Highway*), overlooking Malibu Beach.

Birdie G's

2421 Michigan Avenue • 310-310-3616
www.birdiegsla.com

✓ One of Santa Monica's assets is that it lacks LA pretension. And when it comes to dining, there's no more laid-back yet hip venue than Birdie G's. Tucked away within Santa Monica's historic Bergamot Station (a creative arts complex in the former railway station), acclaimed chef Jeremy Fox's fabulous neighborhood restaurant is named for his daughter (Birdie) and grandma (Gladys). Granny's homespun cooking informs Birdie G's large comfort food-with-a-global-twist menu. The setting is fitting too: a huge sunlit space with lofty industrial ceiling, cement brick walls, and an intimate lounge bar with blue-cushioned booths.

Fox has been playfully off-kilter with granny's muse. Whimsical mashups include a sweet and savory Sloppy Jeremy" on Texas toast, spicy Italian ravioli, beet-and-beef borscht, and Hangtown Brei (soft-scrambled egg topped with matzo, pork belly, fried oysters, and spicy hollandaise). And who can resist the over-the-top Gladys' Lengua Pot Roast—beef tongue with potatoes and carrots accompanied by fried kasha cakes with schmaltz, *gribenes* (crispy chicken skin), chives, spring onions, lemon zest, and aioli? Leave room for classic chocolate layer cake or crème brûlée.

Birdie G's.
(Courtesy Birdie G's)

Nearby Alternatives

Museum: California Heritage Museum

Architecture, culture, and history buffs are all served by this small museum housed in a Queen Anne revival mansion built in 1894 by architect Sumner P. Hunt. The permanent exhibition focuses on photographs, artifacts, and decorative arts from Southern California's past, while upstairs, changing exhibitions range from Hollywood movies to surfing.
2612 Main Street
310-392-8537
www.californiaheritagemuseum.org

Museum: Museum of Flying

This aviation museum at Santa Monica airport pays homage principally to the Douglas Aircraft Company in the early years of commercial and military aviation. Its California Aviation Hall of Fame profiles local aviation visionaries. Your coolest surprise is a full-scale replica of the Wright brothers' *Wright Flyer*, built as a movie prop.
3100 Airport Avenue
310-398-2500
www.museumofflying.org

Outdoors: Venice Beach

Neighboring Santa Monica to the south, bohemian Venice Beach was laid out in 1905 as a mini version of Venice, Italy, with canals and even gondolas. Only a few of the cottage-lined canals remain. Head to Dell Avenue to view them, with their quaint bridges looking more Dutch than Venetian.
310-745-1064
www.visitveniceca.com

Outdoors: Will Rogers State Historic Park

Cowboy-movie star Will Rogers (1879-1935)—the highest-paid actor in 1930s Hollywood—established his 359-acre ranch in the Santa Monica Mountains. Overlooking the Pacific Ocean, his former 31-room ranch house tempts you with stables, corrals, a riding ring, a polo field, and hiking and riding trails that lead into the mountain wilderness.
1501 Will Rogers State Park Road
310-230-2017
www.parks.ca.gov/?page_id=626

Trip Planning

Santa Monica Travel & Tourism
2427 Main Street
310-319-6263
www.santamonica.com

HOLLYWOOD

ALTHOUGH THE MOVIE studios that powered Hollywood to fame are long gone, nowhere else in LA is so tantalizingly associated with stars of the silver screen. The Academy Awards ceremony is still held at the former Kodak Theatre (today the Dolby Theater), not too far from the iconic Chinese Theatre, built in 1927, on Hollywood Boulevard. A visit to Universal Studios (on the *north* side of the Hollywood Hills) is today more of a Disneyland-style experience than a true studio tour. But you can still get a sense for real-life "work on the lot" at Paramount Studios.

Hollywood is packed with other fun things to experience, including the must-do Hollywood Walk of Fame, Hollywood Museum, Hollywood Forever Park Cemetery, and, in West Hollywood, Mel's Drive-In All-American Diner. To the south, the new Academy Museum of Motion Pictures is flanked by the La Brae Tar Pits, Los Angeles County Museum of Art, and the phenomenal Petersen Automotive Museum. Then, you might end your day with a concert at the Hollywood Bowl, beneath the world-famous, #instaready Hollywood sign.

Hollywood Walk of Fame

Hollywood Chamber of Commerce • 6255 Sunset Boulevard, Suite 150
323-469-8311 • www.walkoffame.com

✓ Your rite of passage in Tinseltown should definitely be a stroll along the iconic Hollywood Walk of Fame with its more than 2,700 stars honoring luminaries in live theatre, motion pictures, radio, recording, and television. The five-pointed coral-pink terrazzo and brass-lined stars are embedded in the black sidewalks along 17 blocks of Hollywood Boulevard (between La Brea and Gower) and three blocks of Vine Street (between Yucca and Sunset).

It's fun to walk the 1.5-mile-long Hollywood Walk, seeking out your matinee and entertainment idols, be it **Roger Moore** (whose star is located at 7007 Hollywood Blvd. in salute to his James Bond 007 films) or **Mickey Mouse** (*6925 Hollywood Boulevard*), who became the first fictional character to receive a star in 1978. You can find star locations on the Hollywood Chamber of Commerce's Walk of Fame Directory website.

The original walk with 1,558 stars was completed in spring 1961. An average of two stars are unveiled each month at free public ceremonies attended by honorees—a great way to see a star and their celebrity entourages.

Hollywood Walk of Stars.
(Copyright David Iliff, CC BY-SA 3.0, via Wikimedia Commons)

Petersen Automotive Museum, *Seeing Red* exhibit.
(Courtesy Petersen Automotive Museum)

Petersen Automotive Museum

6060 Wilshire Boulevard
323-930-2277 • www.petersen.org

☑ Automotive heaven! Taking up an entire city block, this trilevel museum along "Museum Row" is chock-full of a mind-boggling assortment of 350-plus vehicles. Most are consequential, from an 1886 Benz (considered the world's first true automobile) to the world's fastest production car—the Bugatti Veyron Grand Sport Vitesse—and an astonishingly wide collection of cars owned by the rich and famous or that appeared in movies. It adds up to one of the most eclectic, if not the finest, ensemble of eye-candy cars in the world.

Two floors of themed exhibitions include *Supercars: A Century of Spectacle and Speed,* displaying iconic race cars of the past 100 years, from a 1913 Mercer Type 35-J Raceabout to such rarities as Steve McQueen's 1955 Jaguar XKSS, built to compete at Le Mans. Finally, explore the basement **Vault**, featuring more than 250 vehicles of cultural significance, from one-of-a-kinds such as the Popemobile to cars that pushed the boundaries of innovation. Emerging in 2015 from a $125 million renovation, its stunning façade of steel ribbons alone is worth the visit.

Musso & Frank Grill

6667 Hollywood Boulevard • 323-467-7788 • www.mussoandfrank.com

☑ Hollywood has many fine restaurants, but you really haven't done Hollywood properly if you haven't dined at Musso & Frank Grill. Claiming to be Hollywood's oldest restaurant, this clubby A-list hangout opened in 1919 and is still run by the original Musso family. Remarkably, even original French chef Jean Rue's classic menu remains relatively unchanged a century later. Back in the day, its storied Back Room was a legendary private space reserved for the Hollywood and literary elite (the Screen Writers Guild is across the street). Deals were made, scripts discussed, novels written, and stars were born (albeit, we assume, not conceived) in its comfortable well-worn red-leather booths.

A martini or other old-school cocktail at the

Musso & Frank Grill, torten.
(Courtesy Musso & Frank Grill)

mahogany bar is reason enough to visit. The all-day breakfast menu (think omelets and pancakes) and extensive lunch and dinner menus of nostalgic dishes are a draw unto themselves. Favorites include chicken potpie, liver and onions, lobster thermidor, grilled lamb kidneys (Charlie Chaplin's favorite), and various Italian dishes. Desserts are equally familiar, from Key Lime pie to New York cheesecake.

Nearby Alternatives

Venue: Paramount Studios

Paramount Studios is the longest-running major film studio still active in Hollywood. Blockbusters from *The Sheik* (1921) to *Titanic* (1997) were filmed here. A fascinating guided two-hour tour grants an intimate behind-the-scenes look inside this working studio, with its iconic show stage sets and extensive backlot.

5515 Melrose Avenue
323-956-1777
www.paramountstudiotour.com

Museum: Los Angeles County Museum of Art

The West Coast's largest art museum has been totally rebuilt in a stunning new building and begs a visit with its globe-crossing collections that cover the full span of history. Strong suits include Asian, Islamic, and Latin American art, the latter including works by Frida Kahlo, Diego Rivera, and José Clemente Orozco.

5905 Wilshire Boulevard
323-857-6000
www.lacma.org

Venue: Universal Studios Hollywood

No matter your age, you'll delight to a behind-the-scenes tour of this world-famous movie studio. Begin by exploring real film sets where Hollywood blockbusters were made. Be enraptured by **The Wizarding World of Harry Potter**. Then hold on tight for a heart-pounding ride on the **Fast & Furious–Supercharged** grand finale.

100 Universal City Plaza
866-959-9688
www.universalstudioshollywood.com

Museum: La Brea Tar Pits

Real tar pits in the heart of metropolitan LA? The tar is still bubbling at the world's only active, urban Ice Age excavation site, where mammoths, saber-toothed cats, giant sloths, and other animals were trapped in sticky asphalt eons ago. You can admire their fossil skeletons in the museum.

5801 Wilshire Boulevard
213-763-3499
www.tarpits.org

Trip Planning

West Hollywood Travel & Tourism Board

1017 North La Cienega Boulevard,
Suite 400
310-289-2525
www.visitwesthollywood.com
www.discoverlosangeles.com

BEVERLY HILLS

TS VERY NAME is synonymous with wealth, luxury, and the celebrity lifestyle. From *The Beverly Hillbillies* and *The Real Housewives of Beverly Hills* TV series to the real-life celebrity lifestyle, the city lives up to its glistening reputation. The hills above Sunset Boulevard are a locus for some of the world's priciest real estate, including the fabulous homes of movie stars and other celebrities.

South of Sunset Boulevard, the "Golden Triangle" bordered by Santa Monica Boulevard, North Crescent Drive, and Wilshire Boulevard, also has plenty of fabulous architectural (and celebrity-centric) venues, including the Spanish colonial Civic Center, the beaux arts-style Beverly Wilshire Hotel, and the old "Pink Palace" (aka Beverly Hills Hotel), which is as glamorous a retreat today as it was in the golden age of Hollywood movies. Plus, Beverly Hills is world renowned for opulent shopping concentrated on Rodeo Drive—ground zero for celebrity-spotting. How can you resist?

Celebrity Home Tour

www.gpsmycity.com • www.bikesandhikesla.com • www.startracktours.com

☑ You may never be able to afford a home in Beverly Hills, but that can't stop you from checking out the real estate of 90210—the quintessential celebrity city's famous zip code. Who in their right mind would *not* want to drive (or even stroll or bicycle) the winding, secluded, woodsy, hillside back roads, in search of spectacular mansions owned—or once owned—by a favorite celebrity? From Hugh Hefner's Playboy Mansion to the lavish estates of Elton John, Ellen DeGeneres, Jay Leno, Jennifer Lopez, Justin Bieber, Kim Kardashian, Madonna, Michael Jackson, Rihanna, and . . . well, it's a long list!

It doesn't take much detective work to compile a list of celebrities' homes and plan a self-guided tour. But for the insider scoop on the architecture, history, and celebrity peccadillos, sign up for a narrated tour with one of the several companies that specialize in celebrity home tours of Beverly Hills. Some will take you are far as ridgecrest in **Mulholland Drive**, where Jack Nicholson, Marlon Brando, and Warren Beatty were once neighbors, earning it the nickname "Bad Boy Drive." With **Classic Experiences** (*www.classicexperiences.com*), you can even be chauffeured in a classic Cadillac.

Celebrity Home Tour. (Courtesy Classic Experiences)

Rodeo Drive, Two Rodeo Drive. (Courtesy Love Beverly Hills)

Rodeo Drive

Rodeo Drive, between Santa Monica Boulevard and Wilshire Boulevard
www.rodeodrive-bh.com

✔ When Giorgio Beverly Hills opened on Rodeo Drive in 1961, other luxury purveyors followed suit. This palm-lined Beverly Hills boulevard soon became ground zero for glamorous shopping. Today, more than 100 of the world's leading luxury brands—from Cartier to Chanel—have stores along the three blocks between Santa Monica Boulevard and Wilshire Boulevard, drawing shopaholic A-list celebrities.

Start at the sumptuous **Beverly Wilshire** hotel—famously a setting for the movie *Pretty Woman*—at Rodeo Drive and Wilshire Boulevard. Next, cross the street and ascend the selfie-ready staircase to **Two Rodeo Drive**, the raised European-style cobblestone piazza with old streetlamps. It curls back down to Dayton Way, where a 14-foot-tall aluminum nude female *Torso* by legendary artist Robert Graham marks the beginning of the Rodeo Drive Walk of Style, with bronze plaques in the sidewalk honoring fashion legends. Don't miss Frank Lloyd Wright's trilevel **Anderton Court** (*330 Rodeo Drive*), or the yellow parking meter reserved for a yellow Bugatti, Rolls Royce, and Aston Martin outside the exclusive **Bijan** men's store (*443 North Rodeo Drive*).

The Grill on the Alley

9560 Dayton Way • 310-276-0615 • www.thegrillonthealley.com/beverly-hills

☑ A classic old-school steakhouse, The Grill on the Alley has been a Beverly Hills power lunch institution for more than three decades. Modeled after a 1930s grill house, the timeless clubby bistro vibe—think elegant hardwood and black-and-white tiled floor, leather banquet booths, and white-jacketed waiters—is more New York City than California. That's until you start spotting on-screen personalities and other movie industry biggies. Plus, being just steps from Rodeo Drive makes this famous dining destination an irresistible spot to break your day over lunch.

Needless to say, the menu is heavy on traditional steakhouse fare, with chops and USDA prime steaks prepared in multitudinous styles. Regardless, they're guaranteed to cut like butter. Other faves include chicken potpie, braised short ribs, poached salmon, and similar fresh fish entrées, plus a delish grilled shrimp pomodoro over angel-hair pasta. Want to go light? Try the crab cake or Grill Cobb Salad. Whatever you choose, be sure to leave room for a signature (and generously portioned) dessert, such as fudge brownie or New York cheesecake. Just be prepared for Rodeo Drive prices.

The Grill on the Alley. (Courtesy The Grill on the Alley)

Nearby Alternatives

Venue: Pacific Design Center

Enormous and enormously colorful sums up the three stunning buildings comprising this massive venue of shops, offices, and exhibition space for all things related to interior design and decor. Located in neighboring West Hollywood, it's worth the short drive to be awed by the entirely blue, green, and red architectural landmarks.

8687 Melrose Avenue
310-657-0800
www.pacificdesigncenter.com

Venue: Greystone Mansion & Gardens

This grandiose English-style country house manor was completed in 1928 for the son of oil tycoon Edward L. Doheny. Today owned by the City of Beverly Hills, the opulently furnished National Register of Historic Places manse and its vast grounds are a public park and popular setting for Hollywood movies.

905 Loma Vista Drive
310-285-6830
www.beverlyhills.org/greystone

Venue: Beverly Hills Hotel

The legendary "Pink Palace" has been Beverly Hills's ultimate beacon of glamour since birthing the city in 1912. Set amid palm-shaded tropical gardens, it harks back to Hollywood's golden age and is still a celebrity hot spot. Sip a Manhattan at the legendary Polo Lounge . . . and keep your eyes peeled (fingers crossed) for one of your favorite TV or on-screen heartthrobs to appear!

9641 Sunset Boulevard
310-276-2251
www.dorchestercollection.com

Restaurant: Spago

Wolfgang Puck's flagship (and recently rejuvenated) restaurant has been top of the Beverly Hills heap for more than 35 years. The VIP-only enclosed patio is sure to be hosting some famous star. The hoi polloi still gets to savor nouveau dishes with an Asian edge in a chic contemporary space.

176 North Canon Drive
310-385-0880
www.wolfgangpuck.com

Trip Planning

Beverly Hills Conference & Visitors Bureau
9400 South Santa Monica Boulevard, #102
310-248-1015
www.lovebeverlyhills.com

ANAHEIM

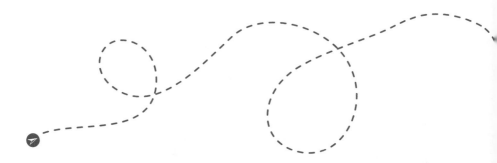

WHILE SAYING "HI!" to Mickey at Disneyland may be the main reason a huge percentage of people visit Anaheim, this large Orange County city has plenty of alternative entertainment. But let's start with the house of the mouse. Anaheim's biggest draw could easily keep you captivated for days. Disneyland and its neighboring sister park, California Adventure, each deserve at least half a day (one day for each is more realistic); by the way, Southern California residents may not know that they're eligible for discounted tickets.

When you're done with all the Disney excitement, you'll find Anaheim's glut of theme parks includes Knott's Berry Farm—the original West Coast theme park. And the Flightdeck Air Combat Simulation Center puts you in the pilot's seat for air-to-air combat at 600 knots. Outdoorsy types can head into the Anaheim Hills for hiking or west to Seal Beach National Wildlife Refuge for birding. Culture vultures will delight in the Bowers Museum. Then there's the Angels Stadium, where you can catch a baseball game with LA's "other" baseball team.

Disneyland Park

1313 Disneyland Drive • 714-781-7290 • disneyland.disney.go.com

☑ Since opening in 1955, Disneyland has been the Happiest Place on Earth, enthralling kids of all ages! The world's most magical theme park offers a full day's worth of fun and excitement, especially when combined with the Disneyland California Adventure Park. Get there early! The early bird gets the shortest lines, which means heading to your preferred rides and attractions first.

Youngsters will thrill to meeting their favorite Disney characters and to such classic Disneyland rides as **Dumbo the Flying Elephant**. With more than 30 themed rides, there's something for everyone. Set sail with the **Pirates of the Caribbean**, or career along a track with the **Indiana Jones Adventure**—just two of Disneyland's nostalgic movie tie-ins. Adrenalin junkies will line up for hours to plummet down a waterfall at **Splash Mountain** or to rocket through the indoor, nearly pitch-black **Space Mountain** coaster. You can also partake in an epic battle on the astoundingly real and exciting new **Star Wars: Rise of the Resistance**—one of several rides for Star Wars fanatics.

Disneyland, Mickey Mouse. (Credit Joshua Sudock; courtesy Disneyland Resort)

Knotts Berry Farm, HangTime. (Courtesy Knotts Berry Farm Marketing)

Knott's Berry Farm

8039 Beach Boulevard • Buena Park • 714-220-5200 • www.knotts.com

☑ California's original theme park dates back to the 1920s, when Walter Knott built a replica Ghost Town as a fun adjunct to his popular roadside berry stand. Knott's Berry Farm has since grown into one of the biggest theme parks in California. It still retains its quaint **Wild West** reconstruction, including a Wild West stunt show. But it has a *really* wild side too. In fact, adrenaline junkies can choose from 40 rides, including scream-inducing roller coasters. First-timers might try the relatively tame **Pony Express**, lacking inversions and huge drops; true addicts get the extreme **Xcelerator**. And the aptly named **Supreme Scream** is a high-speed straight-up, straight-down gravity-defying thrill ride that includes three seconds of total weightlessness!

Camp Snoopy offers a pint-sized roller coaster, water rides, and dozens of other attractions for younger children. Between May and September, the really cool place to be is the adjoining **Knott's Soak City Water Park** (separate entrance fee), with almost two dozen waterslides, plus a lazy river, giant wave pool, and **Gemmie Lagoon**—a scaled-down play area for pint-size tots.

Anaheim Packing House

440 South Anaheim Boulevard • 714-533-7225
www.anaheimpackingdistrict.com

☑ Just one mile northeast of Disneyland Park, the old Anaheim Packing District has been revived as a thriving artsy and culinary enclave in the heart of downtown. At its core is the Anaheim Packing House, which opened in 2014 in a restored 42,000-square-foot citrus packing house dating from 1919. Having metamorphosed into a culinary center, it brings together more than 20 artisan food producers and purveyors in a stylishly retro public market hall setting.

You're spoiled for choice! The skylit two-level venue features a large central atrium surrounded by two dozen or so specialty food stalls and purveyors, with plenty of communal dining porches and patios, including live music. **Adya Fresh Indian Flavors** showcases the seasoned flavors of India. **Healthy Junk** serves vegan pizzas and burgers. **Sweetbird** serves a delish spicy chicken sandwich with smashed potatoes. And the dim-lit and wonderfully moody, Prohibition-inspired **Blind Rabbit** speakeasy is *the* place for killer cocktails. Additional culinary venues are in the nearby **MAKE Building** and the **Packard Building** (a restored Packard car showroom), which includes the **Anaheim Brewery**.

Anaheim Packing House. (Courtesy Visit Anaheim)

Nearby Alternatives

Museum: Bowers Museum

One of California's finest regional museums, this cultural center focuses on the history and diverse cultures of Orange County, plus the fine arts of the indigenous peoples of the Americas, Oceania, and China. Revolving exhibitions have ranged from *Knights in Armor* and *Shackleton's Endurance* to *Evita: Up Close and Personal*.

2002 North Main Street, Santa Ana
714-567-3600
www.bowers.org

Activity: Disneyland California Adventure Park

The California-themed twin to Disneyland Park is as much fun as its older sibling, but focuses on Marvel and Pixar characters for its rides and entertainment. For example, zoom through the desert landscape of **Cars Land**, and team up with Spider-Man and other Marvel superheroes at **Avengers Campus**, new for 2020.

1313 Disneyland Drive
714-781-7290
disneyland.disney.go.com

Activity: Flightdeck Air Combat Simulation Center

Don your flight suit, step into your cockpit, and thrill to the exhilaration of being an F-16 fighter pilot. Or experience the excitement of flying a big Boeing 737 passenger aircraft. Although the sensation of flying is real, you're strapped into flight simulators that mimic takeoffs, landings, and in-air maneuvers.

400 West Disney Way
714-937-1511
www.flightdeck1.com

Outdoors: Seal Beach National Wildlife Refuge

This remnant salt marsh protects what remains of old Anaheim Bay, providing a rare habitat for the endangered California least tern and light-footed clapper rail, plus other migratory birds. The 965-acre refuge is located within the Naval Weapons Station Seal Beach. Join a guided tour on the last Saturday of every month.

800 Seal Beach Boulevard, Building 226
562-598-1024
www.fws.gov/refuge/seal_beach

Trip Planning

Visit Anaheim
2099 South State College Boulevard, Suite 600
714-765-2800
www.visitanaheim.org

PASADENA

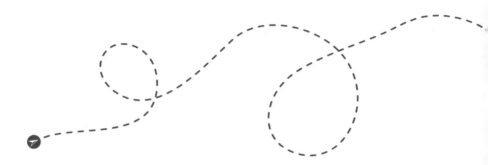

DISTINCTLY HOMEY compared to Hollywood, definitely not as trendy as Santa Monica, and much more highbrow than Anaheim are what make Pasadena—a pretty, wealthy, and relaxed oasis of calm nestled at the base of the San Gabriel Mountains—so enjoyable. Renowned as *the* late 19th-century "millionaire's retreat" in the region, Pasadena boasts fabulous craftsman-style homes, plus a lively, charming, and eminently walkable red-brick Old Town heavy on gastropubs and fine restaurants. Two of California's top cultural centers—The Huntington and the Norton Simon Museum—are here. Space junkies never had it so good, with both the NASA Jet Propulsion Laboratory and Mount Wilson Observatory open to visits. There are also plenty of bucolic retreats, from botanic gardens to hiker-friendly regional parks in the San Gabriel Mountains.

Whether you're spending a day or an entire weekend here, you can't go wrong mixing and matching the following top venues.

The Huntington

1151 Oxford Road • San Marino • 626-405-2100 • www.huntington.org

✓ Eclectic and stunning best describe this must-visit Southern California cultural destination that ranks among North America's finest and kid-friendliest artsy venues. Housed in the former estate of railroad magnate Henry E. Huntington (1850–1927), it provides for a beautiful day of art admiration in a palatial mansion and exploration among 12 themed gardens spread throughout 120 acres.

Officially known as The Huntington Library, Art Museum, and Botanical Garden, it offers a fine triptych that spans rare books and manuscripts, famous works of art, and globe-crossing botanical treasures. There's a lot of ground to cover, but audio tours make things easy. The not-to-miss exhibits include an original Gutenberg Bible, an illuminated manuscript of Chaucer's *The Canterbury Tales*, and a First Folio edition of Shakespeare. The art gallery's top draw is Thomas Gainsborough's iconic *The Blue Boy*.

Start your garden tour in the picturesque **Chinese Garden**, and then take the rest of the morning to explore the Australian, California, Japanese, desert, jungle, and palm gardens. Kids in tow? The **Conservatory** has a children's garden with miniature mazes.

The Huntington, Chinese Garden-Pavilion of The Three Friends.
(Courtesy The Huntington)

NASA Jet Propulsion Laboratory, Mars Rover. (Courtesy NASA JPL-Caltech)

NASA Jet Propulsion Laboratory

4800 Oak Grove Drive
818-354-1234 • www.jpl.nasa.gov

☑ You don't need to be a Trekkie to salivate over an opportunity to get the inside scoop on space exploration. If you're curious as to where the data transmitted by spacecraft is received or who builds the Mars rovers and space robots, then don't pass on a chance to visit NASA's Jet Propulsion Laboratory, the US's leading center for robotic exploration of the solar system and beyond. This huge facility at the base of the San Gabriel Mountains offers free and fascinating—and in high demand—tours that open a whole new universe of understanding about space exploration. (You must submit your request at least three weeks in advance. Alas, only US citizens can apply.)

Your visit begins with a multimedia presentation—"Journey to the Planets and Beyond"—at the **Von Karman Visitor's Center**, displaying full-scale replicas of the *Galileo* spacecraft and Mars rovers. Yes, you'll then see inside the **Space Flight Operations Center** (Mission Control), where NASA engineers communicate with spacecraft. Plus, you'll get to witness the next generation of spacecraft being built.

Café Santorini

64 West Union Street • 626-564-4200 • www.cafesantorini.com

☑ Old Town Pasadena has earned a reputation for some of greater Los Angeles's finest restaurants, which tend to come and go. Now in its fourth decade, Café Santorini is one of the oldest and is still going strong—for good reason. This intimate and elegant red-brick bistro metaphorically transports you to the Mediterranean with its mouthwatering menu specializing in classics such as moussaka, cioppino, and Moroccan lamb shank, plus wood-fired pizzas, hearty pastas, creamy risottos, and small appetizer dishes called mezes (appetizer platters) served family style. The plump grape leaves stuffed with succulent rice and herbs are simply too divine to resist! And you're welcomed with a basket of warm savory bread, made with herbs and served fresh from the oven.

Although the indoor dining room is plenty cozy and made more charming by its raised wooden warehouse-style roof, try to snag a seat on the romantic second-floor rooftop patio. Café Santorini boasts an extensive wine list and a full bar famous for such signature cocktails as Peruvian Heat, spiced up with homemade habanero syrup.

Café Santorini balcony. (Courtesy Café Santorini)

Nearby Alternatives

Venue: Mission San Gabriel Arcángel

One of 21 California missions founded by Spanish friars, Moorish style Mission San Gabriel Arcángel—founded in 1771—is architecturally distinct and richly rewards a visit. Although the church was badly damaged by a fire in July 2020, the altar, bell tower, and museum with its precious artifacts were spared.

**428 South Mission Drive, San Gabriel
626-457-3035
www.missionscalifornia.com**

Museum: Norton Simon Museum

The artists on permanent display at this sensational art museum reads like an A-list of 19th- and 20th-century greats—Botticelli, Degas, Gauguin, Rembrandt, Renoir, Braque, Picasso, and Andy Warhol—all amassed by industrialist billionaire Norton Simon (1907–1993). You'll also marvel at the huge collection of Indian and Southeast Asian art.

**411 West Colorado Boulevard
626-449-6840
www.nortonsimon.org**

Outdoors: Descanso Gardens

A marvelous bucolic urban retreat, Descanso Gardens delights nature lovers with its nine specialized botanical collections, including a rose garden, plus California native plants and oak woodlands, and even a redwood forest. Kids get to ride on a miniature train. And there's a museum, art gallery, and guided weekend walks.

**1418 Descanso Drive, La Cañada Flintridge
818-949-4200
www.descansogardens.org**

Venue: Mount Wilson Observatory

Located atop Mount Wilson, some 10 miles northeast of Pasadena, Mount Wilson Observatory once held the world's largest telescopes, accounting for many stunning cosmological discoveries. It's open for visits daily, and twice-daily docent-led tours are offered on weekends, providing a fascinating perspective on the scientific work that still goes on.

**Mount Wilson Road, La Cañada Flintridge
562-413-2950
www.mtwilson.edu**

Trip Planning

**300 East Green Street
626-793-2122
www.visitpasadena.com
www.oldpasadena.org**

PALM SPRINGS

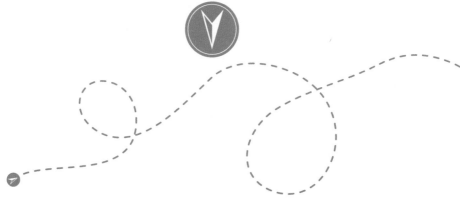

PALM SPRINGS, TWO hours inland of Los Angeles, lures visitors to bask in year-round sunshine, lush palm oases, hot mineral springs, and serene mountain landscapes. Beginning in the 1930s, the arrival of Hollywood stars and starlets turned the sleepy desert outpost into a world-famous retreat and epicenter of Hollywood hedonism. Today, recently reenergized Palm Springs exudes a whole new contemporary cool.

There's no shortage of fun, fascinating, and frolicsome things to do in this chic desert oasis, where *Mad Men*–era retro reigns, and it's the swinging sixties all over again. The dining is fabulous, the spas are among California's best, and this haven even boasts ritzy casinos. Museums cater to aviation buffs, art fans, and nature lovers keen to learn about desert ecology. Plus, nowhere else in California can you cross-country ski in the morning, play golf in the afternoon, and relax outside with an iced martini in the evening.

Modernist Homes of the Rich and Famous

Palm Springs Celebrity Tour • 4741 East Palm Canyon Drive
760-895-8005 • www.palmspringscelebritytours.com

✔ Even before World War II, Palm Springs was a glamorous getaway and playground for movie stars, Hollywood moguls, and plutocrat families. After World War II, when the modernist movement took hold, the city became modernism's place in the sun, not least because the town's fully-fledged flourishing from the 1940s to the go-go 1960s coincided with the explosion of Atomic Age architecture. Scores of the rich and famous—from Frank Sinatra to blonde bombshell Marilyn Monroe—bought ground-hugging modernist homes for their parties and peccadillos.

Whether you cycle, opt for a self-drive itinerary, or join a guided group tour, a celebrity tour is easy to follow, as most homes of Hollywood icons are concentrated in the contiguous Movie Colony, Little Tuscany, and Las Palmas districts. Don't miss the iconic **Tramway Oasis gas station**, Donald Wexler's **steel houses**, the **Kaufmann House**, Elvis Presley's **"Honeymoon House"**, Leonardo DiCaprio's (originally **Dinah Shore's**) estate home, and Frank Sinatra's **"Twin Palms"** (you'll have to rent it to see inside). Leave time to browse fashionably kitsch 1950s home decor at the retro-themed shops on North Palm Canyon Drive.

Modernist homes of the rich and famous. (Courtesy Greater Palm Springs CVB)

Palm Springs Aerial Tramway. (Courtesy Palm Springs CVB)

Palm Springs Aerial Tramway

One Tram Way • 888-515-8726 • www.pstramway.com

☑ The physical setting of Palm Springs is out of this world. Majestic mountains soar on three sides, glistening with snow in the winter sunshine. For a bird's-eye view over the city (and to escape the afternoon heat in midsummer), take a thrilling ride aboard the Palm Springs Aerial Tramway. The world's second-steepest trams rotate 360 degrees as they ascend and descend through four life zones—equivalent to a road trip from Mexico to Alaska in 10 minutes!

At the **Mountain Station** (8,516 feet), the air is some 30°F cooler than the desert below. You're now in **Mount San Jacinto State Park**—a pristine alpine wilderness topped by **Mount San Jacinto** (10,834 feet). The 54 miles of trails include the easy **Desert View Trail**, a 1.5-mile loop that leads to scenic lookouts with vistas over Palm Springs and the Coachella Valley. During winter, you can even rent cross-country skis and snowshoes at the **Long Valley Ranger Station**, a short walk from the Mountain Station. More demanding trails to Mount San Jacinto summit require permits for overnight camping.

Cheeky's

622 North Palm Canyon Way
760-327-7595 • www.cheekysps.com

☑ With good reason, any locals will tell you this casual modern café (open Thursday–Monday, 8 a.m.–2 p.m.) is *the* breakfast and brunch spot in town, as the frequent long lines attest. Situated in the heart of the hip Uptown Design District (close to all those modernist celebrity homes), it has cozy albeit limited interior seating. But the shaded (and, in winter, heated) hedged patio is the place to be.

The menu at Tara Lazar's farm-to-table restaurant changes weekly, making the most of seasonal products. Still, you're guaranteed that the much-buzzed signature Bacon Flight— yes, just various types of bacon!—will be there to highlight the creative and divine comfort food dishes conjured from sometimes quirky combinations ambrosial with flavors. Maybe you'll have French toast with red currants and mascarpone. *Huevos rancheros* never tasted so good. And the house-made maple sage sausage, pesto fries, and corn pancake all rise to the level of heavenly. Other than the Bacon Flight, most dishes are health conscious.

If you can't snag a seat, Cheeky's neighbors include a fistful of other great eateries within a stone's throw.

Cheeky's.
(Courtesy Cheeky's)

Nearby Alternatives

Museum: Palm Springs Art Museum

Housed in an architecturally stunning modernist building, this acclaimed museum has outstanding collections of Native American crafts, classic Western and plein air paintings, plus art from throughout Africa, Asia, and Mesoamerica. Its contemporary glass art (including works by Dale Chihuly) is a highlight, and don't miss the outside sculpture garden and 26-foot-tall **Forever Marilyn** statue.

101 Museum Drive
760-325-7186
www.psmuseum.org

Outdoors: Indian Canyons

Beloved by hikers, three Indian Canyons scythe into the rugged slopes of Mount San Jacinto. Fed by natural springs, stands of California fan palms shade the canyon floors, providing shelter for bobcats, coyotes, and deer. Agua Caliente Indians once lived in the canyons; ancient petroglyphs can be seen while hiking.

South Palm Canyon Drive
760-325-3400
www.indian-canyons.com

Venue: Agua Caliente Cultural Center

Completed in early 2022, the stunning Agua Caliente Cultural Center features a museum dedicated to the history and culture of the local Agua Caliente Band of Cahuilla Indians. Its Spa at Séc-he stands atop hot mineral springs that feed outdoor thermal pools and a green belt replicating the Indian Canyons.

Tahquitz Canyon Way and North Indian Canyon Drive
844-772-2224
www.accmuseum.org

Museum: Palm Springs Air Museum

This living history museum boasts one of the world's largest collections of World War II aircraft; airworthy planes include a P-51 Mustang, P-47 Thunderbolt, and B-17 Flying Fortress. An F-4 Phantom and MiG-21 are highlights in the Korean War and Vietnam War hangar. Flight demonstrations are offered on Saturday afternoons, November through May.

745 North Gene Autry Trail
760-778-6262
www.palmspringsairmuseum.org

Trip Planning

Palm Springs Visitor Center

2901 North Palm Canyon Drive
760-778-8418
www.visitpalmsprings.com

SANTA BARBARA

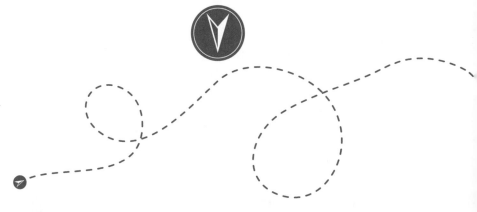

B ILLING ITSELF AS "The American Riviera," this California version of St. Tropez truly does boast a perfect Mediterranean climate and fabulous beaches. Plus, its elegant Spanish colonial revival buildings, laid-back surf culture, and sensational palm-lined setting at the foot of the Santa Ynez Mountains have long made it a glamorous destination for the rich and famous.

From its iconic Mission Santa Barbara—called the "Queen of the Missions" for its picturesque setting and beauty—to its variety of downtown museums and early Spanish-era adobes, it's hard to think of another destination that offers so much. Then there's the landmark Stearns Wharf, cusped by white-sand beaches and the Pacific Ocean, with heaps of kid-friendly adventures. Santa Barbara's sublime wine country—just a short drive away—beckons with a genuine Danish village, hot-air ballooning, horseback riding trails, and plenty of wineries and gourmet restaurants. Here are our recommendations for a perfect day.

Red Tile Walking Tour

santabarbaraca.com/itinerary/red-tile-walking-tour/

☑ Spanish colonial architecture with stucco adobes, red-tiled roofs, and flower-bedecked courtyards is *the* defining element of historic Santa Barbara. Every first-time visitor should lace up comfy shoes and follow the self-guided Red Tile Walking Tour, published by the Santa Barbara Convention & Visitors Bureau. Starting at the **Santa Barbara County Courthouse**, your clockwise route takes in more than 20 adobes from the 18th and 19th centuries, plus 20th-century Spanish-Moorish architectural masterpieces concentrated in just seven blocks (between State and Santa Barbara Streets, and Ortego and Anapamu Streets).

Highlights include the **Santa Barbara Museum of Art** (*www.sbma.net*), **Santa Barbara Historical Museum**, elegant Spanish-style **Public Library**, **Casa De la Guerra** (built between 1819 and 1827 by Presidio comandante José de la Guerra), **Presidio Avenue** (the oldest street in Santa Barbara), former Presidio parade grounds (now a garden), a fistful of charming Spanish adobes, and the reconstructed **Presidio Chapel** clustered close together around **El Presidio de Santa Barbara State Historic Park**. Returning up Anacapa Street, you'll end with the city's Spanish art deco–style **Main Post Office** and the 19th-century **Lobero Theatre**.

Santa Barbara Courthouse. (Credit Blake Bronstad; courtesy Santa Barbara CVB)

Stearns Wharf. (Credit Gabriela Herman; courtesy Santa Barbara CVB)

Stearns Wharf

State Street and Cabrillo • 805-564-5518 • www.stearnswharf.org

☑ Santa Barbara's most iconic landmark is the perfect spot to take in the salty breezes and admire the postcard views along the coastline. Built in 1872 by John P. Stearns as a shipping pier, today this tourist boardwalk attraction is a favored spot for fishers to cast a line. Gear up at **Stearns Wharf Bait & Tackle**. Plus, you'll discover all kinds of treats at **Mother Stearns Candy Shop**. The **Great Pacific Ice Cream Company** sells delicious sherbets and double-scoop ice cream in waffle cones, and the **Coastal Winery** lets you sample the best local wines.

The highlight, however, is the bi-level **Santa Barbara Museum of Natural History Sea Center** (*www.sbnature.org/visit/sea-center*), with life-size mom and baby California gray whales suspended from the ceiling. Kids can get their hands wet in the two-finger touch tanks, populated with rays, sea stars, sharks, and other marine life from the Santa Barbara Channel. Next, take a fun 15-minute narrated boat ride aboard *Lil' Toot*, Santa Barbara's original waterfront taxi, which putters between Stearns Wharf and Santa Barbara Harbor every half hour.

Brophy Bros.

119 Harbor Way • 805-966-4418
www.brophybros.com

☑ There's a good reason—well, several actually—why this seafood restaurant with a to-be-expected nautical motif is hyper-popular. For starters, it's harborside on the marina with stunning views through large bay windows over the water and fishing boats, with the majestic Santa Ynez Mountains beyond. Better yet, sit out on the open-air deck! Then there's the fresh-off-the-boat seafood, including the restaurant's coveted clam chowder.

The huge menu also includes contemporary American cuisine. But you're really here for the seafood, including daily specials that vary from season to season. How about blackened seabass dusted in Cajun spices, Chilean snow crab, or seafood pasta with gulf shrimp and sea scallops. Maybe you'll have sautéed ahi breaded with roasted cashews or grilled mahi mahi with mango-papaya relish. All entrées are served with coleslaw and a choice of rice pilaf or French fries and salad or chowder. And, yes, if you're wondering . . . Brophy's *does* serve beer-battered fish and chips! You can also belly up to the raw oyster and clam bar. Brophy's doesn't take reservations, but any wait is worth it.

Brophy Bros.
seafood. (Courtesy
Brophy Bros.)

Nearby Alternatives

Venue: Mission Santa Barbara

As the "Queen of the Missions," Old Mission Santa Barbara is among California's most beautiful of the 21 missions. Established by Spanish Franciscans in 1786, it is still a practicing mission. Don't miss the cemetery and lush rose garden. Take a guided tour to learn about its art, architecture, and history.
2201 Laguna Street
805-682-4149
www.santabarbaramission.org

Museum: The Wolf Museum of Exploration + Innovation (MOXI)

Curious minds of all ages get to ignite their synapses at this interactive museum where hands-on experiences span seven themes related to science, technology, and the arts. Kiddos can build their own car to race on a speed track or even design an invention to create with a 3D printer.
25 State Street
805-770-5000
www.moxi.org

Venue: Solvang

A 45-minute drive from Santa Barbara, this genuine Danish village nestled in the Santa Ynez Valley is as Scandinavian today as when it was founded in 1911. The "Danish Capital of America" has its windmill, rooftop storks, and other quintessential Danish architecture, plus great bakeries, restaurants, and wine-tasting rooms.
Solvang Conference and Visitors Bureau
1637 Copenhagen Drive
805-688-6144
www.solvangusa.com

Activity: Hot-Air Ballooning

Embark on a spectacular sky-high adventure above the Santa Ynez Valley wine country at **Los Olivos**, a 45-minute drive northwest of Santa Barbara. The tranquility and the scenery of vineyards and rolling green hills below will take your breath away. This soaring adventure is a perfect sunrise or sunset experience.
2432 Railway Avenue, Suite A, Los Olivos
760-602-0295
www.skysthelimitballooning.com

Trip Planning

Santa Barbara Convention & Visitors Bureau
500 East Montecito Street
805-966-9222
www.santabarbaraca.com

SAN LUIS OBISPO

ONE OF CALIFORNIA'S most endearingly overlooked destinations, this Central Coast university town is one of its most charming urban enclaves, with a fabulously preserved historic core. It's a something-for-everyone city. Yes, there's a superbly preserved 18th-century mission founded by Father Junipero Serra. The San Luis Obispo Museum of Art displays impressive contemporary Californian art. There's also a kid's museum, plus such quirky sites as Bubblegum Alley, which is exactly as you may imagine! Hikers can ascend trails up Bishop Peak. And just when you thought downtown couldn't get any more charming, the classic cable car–style trolley rolls by (Thursdays to Sundays).

No wonder it's such a popular halfway stopping point between Big Sur and Santa Barbara. And nestled in the foothills of the Santa Lucia Mountains, a 15-minute drive inland of the coast, it makes a great base for exploring such surrounding attractions as Pismo Beach, Morro Bay, and—above all—Hearst Castle.

Hearst Castle

750 Hearst Castle Road • San Simeon • 800-444-4445 • hearstcastle.org

☑ One of California's top tourist venues, the iconic Hearst Castle is America's most extravagant château. High atop the Santa Lucia Mountains, the former estate of multimillionaire newspaper tycoon William Randolph Hearst, with its 165-room villa by Julia Morgan, is not to be missed. This astonishing, and truly palatial, mountaintop estate is the jewel in the crown of the region. Visits are by guided tours only (specialist theme tours are an option) by reservations: book well in advance. In Spring and Autumn, a special evening tour lets you experience Hearst Castle at twilight.

When Hearst commissioned "Miss Morgan" to build him "a little something," the result was California's finest architectural showpiece of the era. Highlights include the **Neptune Pool**, reminiscent of ancient Rome; the indoor mosaic-tiled **Roman Pool**, replete with marble statues of Roman gods and goddesses; and the Tudor-style **Assembly Room**, with its original 16th-century tapestries and where you sense King Henry VIII would feel at home. And if you think you spot zebras wandering the surrounded mountains, you do! They're a legacy of Hearst's personal zoo.

Hearst Castle. (Copyright Christopher P. Baker)

Pismo Beach. (Copyright Christopher P. Baker)

Pismo Beach

Visitor Information Center • 581 Dolliver Street • 805-556-7397
www.experiencepismobeach.com

☑ California's Central Coast has year-round allure. The laid-back seaside town of Pismo Beach, with its 23-mile-long stretch of shoreline, ticks all the boxes. Surfers and bodyboarders love it for consistent beach breaks, kitesurfers for its consistent winds, and scuba divers for its plentiful marine life and warm waters. Winter is prime time to head out on a half-day whale-watching expedition (although humpback whales can be seen in these waters 365 days a year). Monarch butterflies flutter in by their tens of thousands throughout winter months to settle in the eucalyptus and pine trees of **Monarch Butterfly Grove**.

The Grove is part of **Pismo State Beach**, which unfurls south to **Oceano Dunes**—a vast expanse of dunes designated as a Special Vehicle Recreation Area for you to go wild and kick up sand in your ATV or off-road vehicle. If relaxation is more your thing, stroll (or cast a line from) the picture-perfect public fishing pier, and then head to the north end of the beach where the scenic sea stacks and craggy bluffs are colored by seasonal wildflowers.

Novo

726 Higuera Street
805-543-3986 • www.novorestaurant.com

✓ *Wine Enthusiast* knows a thing or two about fine restaurants, so naming Novo one of America's 100 Best Wine Restaurants is a trustworthy recommendation. Novo's wine list includes plenty of premium local and globe-spanning labels. That's fitting, as this artsy and romantic restaurant and lounge in an old cigar warehouse serves internationally inspired cuisine ranging from Mexico and the Mediterranean to Thailand and Japan, with ever-variable seasonal ingredient-driven menus highlighting a few select mouthwatering treats at a time.

Executive Chef Ben Richardson conjures an unbelievable potpourri of diverse dishes, from locally sourced beef and vegetarian burgers to salmon bisque, Singapore satay, pork *sopes,* and Moroccan fried chicken. Vegetarians will find plenty of vegan and gluten-free options. And the ethnic cuisine can be paired to sakes, tequilas, and an international A-list of bottled beers. The homemade ice cream desserts made from local sheep's milk are reason enough to make a beeline. The same can be said for the popular and leisurely Sunday brunch. Reservations are essential, especially to snag a table on the patio deck overlooking tree-shaded San Luis Obispo Creek.

Novo Restaurant patio. (Courtesy Novo Restaurant)

Nearby Alternatives

Activity: Downtown Walking Tour

San Luis Obispo's downtown has heaps of eclectic sites and fascinating buildings packed along five short blocks of Monterey Street and Higuera Street. Don't miss old **Mission San Luis Obispo de Tolosa**, the **San Luis Obispo Museum of Art**, and **Bubblegum Alley**, which is plastered with countless pieces of chewed bubblegum.

San Luis Obispo Visitor Center
895 Monterey Street
877-756-8696
www.slocal.com

Venue: Morro Bay

This traditional fishing town with a still-active fleet is one of the country's top destinations for birding and a great place for spotting dolphins, seals, and otters. This peaceful seaside town exudes an irresistible charm enhanced by shoreline state parks and fantastic sea-kayaking around an ancient volcanic plug—Morro Rock.

695 Harbor Street, Morro Bay
805-225-7411
www.morrobay.org

Venue: Lompoc & Mission La Purísima Concepción

Offbeat Lompoc, a one-hour drive south from San Luis Obispo, offers a tremendous twofer. Begin with its outdoor mural walk in **Old Town**, where some 40 murals portray local history. The Visitors Bureau has a map at *www.explorelompoc. com*. Round out your visit with nearby **La Purísima Mission State Historic Park**.

Lompoc Valley Chamber of Commerce & Visitors Bureau
111 South I Street, Lompoc
805-736-4567
www.explorelompoc.com
La Purísima Mission State Historic Park
2295 Purisima Road, Lompoc
805-733-3713
www.lapurisimamission.org

Activity: Bishop Peak

One of the tallest of the nine *morros* ("the nine sisters"—rounded volcanic cones) surrounding San Luis Obispo, Bishop Peak looms to the city's northwest. You can hike the popular Bishop Peak Trail to the summit, which has an official rock-climbing area. It's about three miles round trip.
www.slocountyparks.com/ trails/bishop-peak-natural-area

Trip Planning

San Luis Obispo Visitor Center
895 Monterey Street
877-756-8696
www.slocal.com

MONTEREY

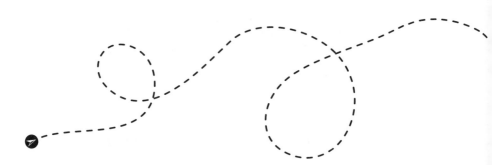

IT'S HARD TO think of a comparably compact coastal community with so much to offer. "Monterey" comprises the cities of Monterey, Carmel-by-the-Sea, Pebble Beach, and the rugged Big Sur coastline—nowhere in California surpasses it for rugged grandeur. The Monterey Bay Aquarium—located on the historic and revitalized Cannery Row—is an absolute must. Plus, you simply have to walk Old Fisherman's Wharf and nearby Monterey State Historic Park, with its well-preserved buildings dating back to before Monterey became California's first capital.

Just a short distance from town, Carmel-by-the-Sea—as quaint and chic a seaside village as can be—boasts one of California's finest Spanish missions. Nearby, some of the world's best golf courses await in Pebble Beach, with its stellar 17-Mile Drive. Further south, there's the wildlife of Point Lobos State Natural Reserve, plus the epic scenery of Big Sur. Oh, and let's not forget the Steinbeck Museum in Salinas.

Monterey Historic State Park

Pacific House Museum • 20 Custom House Plaza
831-649-2907 • www.parks.ca.gov/?page_id=575

☑ Monterey served as California's capital under Spanish, Mexican, and, finally, US rule when the US flag was officially raised in California here on July 7, 1846. Immediately south of Old Fisherman's Wharf is Old Monterey—a collection of significant historic buildings comprising Monterey State Historic Park. You can arrange a guided history tour or download a brochure with map off the park website for a self-guided walk.

Begin at the **Custom House** and **Pacific House Museum/ Interpretive Visitor Center**. From here, the two-mile "Monterey Walking Path of History" follows a logical route, guided by yellow-tiled markers as you step into the past. Twelve key sites (out of 55 in total) include the oldest government building in California; sturdy adobe residences, such as **Cooper-Molera Adobe** and **Casa Soberanes**; the **Robert Louis Stevenson House**; and **Colton Hall**, site of the state's first constitutional convention. And don't miss the whalebone sidewalks and **Old Whaling Station**. The route also takes you past the **Monterey Museum of Art** (*559 Pacific Street, www.montereyart.org*), displaying many works by California and local artists.

Monterey Historic State Park, Colton Hall. (Copyright Christopher P. Baker)

Monterey Bay Aquarium.
(Copyright Christopher P. Baker)

Monterey Bay Aquarium

886 Cannery Row • 831-648-4800 • www.montereybayaquarium.org

✓ The Pacific waters off Monterey teem with marine creatures great and small. Seeing the sea life is made easy by this huge aquarium, world-renowned for the grand scale of its stunning interactive exhibits. Housed in a former sardine cannery, the sunlit aquarium boasts more than 35,000 sea creatures representing 600-plus species. Many visitors come just to see the sea otters—Monterey's furry homegrown mammalian mascot—playing in their two-story exhibit.

You can also view live bluefin and yellowfin tuna, plus jellyfish, Pacific octopi, hammerhead sharks, stingrays, and even seahorses and sunfish below the waterline. Many can be viewed swimming in the massive 1.2-million-gallon **Open Sea** exhibit through one of the world's largest single-pane sheets of glass. Don't miss the **Kelp Forest**, the Splash Zone's **Coral Reef Kingdom**, the swirling school of sardines, the behind-the-scenes tours, and, especially, the otter, sea lion, and South African penguin feeding times! Plenty of children-specific exhibits, such as touch pools, keep kids enthralled. The tropical fish tank lets them spot Nemo's cousins. There's even a waterbed for making waves!

Passionfish

701 Lighthouse Avenue • Pacific Grove
831-655-3311 • www.passionfish.net

☑ Passionfish is renowned as a pioneer of the sustainable seafood movement and was the first officially certified "Green" restaurant in Monterey County. In the heart of chic Pacific Grove and just steps from the entrance to 17-Mile Drive, this elegantly contemporary restaurant with leather banquet seating offers a truly California dining experience that fits perfectly with the nearby Monterey Aquarium's focus on saving our oceans. That means the freshest sustainable seafood, conscientiously fished (overfished species aren't even considered). Such abundant—and or farmed—species as sablefish and sturgeon are staples on an ever-variable menu.

Chef Ted Walters' signature recipes have been featured in *Bon Appetit* magazine and several top-selling cookbooks, as well as on the Discovery Health Channel. In autumn, fresh, farmed sturgeon might be served over jasmine rice with a side of organic lemongrass slaw tossed in a spicy red curry vinaigrette. Or maybe you'd prefer fresh-caught sea scallops drizzled with tomato-truffle butter, a basil-stuffed rainbow trout, or organic greens salad lustily loaded with fresh tender crab and avocado, with ginger vinaigrette adding spice?

Passionfish, striped bass crudo. (Courtesy Passionfish)

Nearby Alternatives

Activity: Carmel-by-the-Sea

A stone's throw south of Monterey, this enchanting petite town of whimsical cottages evolved as a wealthy bohemian enclave. Spilling down to a cliff-cusped beach, it boasts dozens of art galleries, chic restaurants and tea rooms, and the perfectly preserved **Mission San Carlos Borroméo del Rio Carmelo,** founded in 1771.

Carmel Chamber of Commerce Visitor Center
Carmel Plaza Ocean Avenue, between Junipero and Mission
831-624-2522
www.carmelcalifornia.com

Museum: Steinbeck Museum

Head east to John Steinbeck's hometown of Salinas and its Steinbeck Museum, which celebrates the life and work of the Nobel Prize-winning author. It's full of rare artifacts and interactive multisensory exhibits, including rooms dedicated to showcasing *Cannery Row, The Grapes of Wrath*, and so on.

1 Main Street • 831-775-4721
www.steinbeck.org

Activity: Point Lobos State Natural Reserve

Find inspiration at this coastal reserve, which protects archeological sites, unique geological formations, rich flora, and a wealth of fauna, including seals, sea lions, sea otters, migrating gray whales (December–May), and flocks of seabirds. Don't miss the 19th-century cabin built by Chinese fishermen at **Whalers Cove**.

Highway 1, 3 miles south of Carmel-by-the-Sea
813-624-4909
www.parks.ca.gov/?page_id=571

Activity: 17-Mile Drive and Big Sur

One of America's most astounding scenic drives, the pay-to-enter 17-mile perimeter road (open from sunrise to sunset) offers jaw-dropping coastal vistas, the world-famous **Lone Cypress**, seals and sea lions, and iconic golf courses. Now up the ante tenfold by continuing south along the **Big Sur** coastline!

Pebble Beach Visitor Center
1700 17-Mile Drive
866-876-3130
www.pebblebeach.com/17-mile-drive

Trip Planning:

Monterey County Convention & Visitors Bureau
419 Webster Street, Suite 100
888-221-1010
www.seemonterey.com

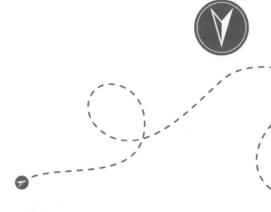

SANTA CRUZ

A DARLING OF TRAVELERS, this quintessential California beach town is synonymous with sand, surf, and summer fun. The Central Coast shoreline hideaway and its redwood-forested mountain surrounds are absolutely bursting with fabulous things to see and do. It's logical to head straight for the fun-filled Boardwalk seaside amusement park, with its iconic roller coaster and then to the adjacent wharf, with its resident population of sea lions. The nearby Monterey Bay National Marine Sanctuary Exploration Center educates with fabulous exhibits.

Next, you can choose to stroll Santa Cruz's charming downtown, check out its historic mission, take a scenic cliff-top walk along West Cliff Drive and watch surfers ride crashing waves beside the Surfing Museum, or drive the gorgeous coastline to Capitola and Natural Bridges State Park with its monarch butterfly grove. And how about a ride on an old-fashioned steam train through the redwood forests at Roaring Camp Railroad?

Santa Cruz Beach Boardwalk & Wharf

400 Beach Street · 831-423-5590 · www.beachboardwalk.com

☑ This twofer pretty much defines Santa Cruz and is the almost obligatory way to fill your morning. Start at the Santa Cruz Beach Boardwalk—one of the oldest amusement parks in California. Choose from a menu that ranges from calm kiddie rides to thrillers designed for adrenalin junkies. You simply *must* ride the **Giant Dipper**, the park's famed wooden roller coaster that features in such movies as *Sudden Impact*, *The Lost Boys*, and *Dangerous Minds*—it's been a visitor favorite since it was built in 1924, from the first exhilarating dip to the poised slow turn at the top of the million-dollar view.

Now stroll west along the beach to walk the wooden centenarian wharf. Extending exactly a half mile into the **Monterey Bay National Marine Sanctuary**, the US's longest wooden pier reaches into an intertidal zone perfect for spotting dolphins and whales; telescopes stud the pier for zoom-in viewing. Resident seals and sea lions haul themselves out on the structure. To learn more about them, check out the **Monterey Bay National Marine Sanctuary Exploration Center** (*www.montereybay.noaa.gov*), facing the wharf.

Santa Cruz Boardwalk and Wharf. (Courtesy Santa Cruz Beach Boardwalk)

Roaring Camp Railroad. (Copyright Christopher P. Baker)

Roaring Camp Railroad

5401 Graham Hill Road, Felton • 831-335-4484 • www.roaringcamp.com

✓ Head into the Santa Cruz Mountains above town to Felton and the Roaring Camp, an authentic old rail depot that once served the redwood lumbering industry. The "camp" recreates the yesteryear ambience with an 1880s-style general store, museum, train station, and mechanics workshop, as well as several narrow-gauge steam locomotives dating back to 1890. Now hop aboard the **Redwood Forest Steam Train** (daily) for a one-hour ride through towering redwood groves and over 19th-century wooden trestles as it winds up a narrow-gauge grade to the summit of Bear Mountain. Conductors narrate the history of the railroad, lumbering era, and Roaring Camp.

On weekends, you can ride the **Santa Cruz Beach Train** (a General Electric diesel), which heads down the scenic San Lorenzo River Gorge and through Henry Cowell Redwoods State Park before arriving at the Santa Cruz Beach Boardwalk. Don't worry about having to hike back up for your car: Round trips are offered four times daily. You can also hop aboard at the Boardwalk for the round-trip ride, with time to explore the depot.

Kianti's Pizza & Pasta Bar

1100 Pacific Avenue • 831-469-4400 • www.kiantis.com

☑ Sunlit through floor to ceilings walls of glass, this heart-of-downtown restaurant has been voted a "Best of Santa Cruz" dining option for good reason. Maybe it's because any day of the week, your pasta or oven-crisped pizza comes hand-tossed. Or perhaps it's the fun gravity-defying pizza-spinning performances—a true "wow the patrons" show!—by competing staff from the flame-raising open kitchen as the lights go down on Friday and Saturday nights. In fact, there's always a festive mood at this colorful and lively local favorite.

Owners Kelly Kissee and Tracy Parks-Barber favor family-style Italian cooking, such as hand-formed meatballs, pasta dishes smothered with garlic cream sauce, and create-your-own pizzas with more than 30 topping options, from mushrooms and almonds to spicy chicken and spinach, or Italian sausage and garlic. And the huge calzones are bursting with flavorful pepperoni and stringy cheese. The indoor decor is urban-contemporary and includes a full bar with tall stools, but you can opt for the roadside patio, with shade umbrellas in summer and heat lamps in winter.

Kianti's pizza.
(Courtesy Kianti's)

Nearby Alternatives

Outdoors: Natural Bridges State Beach

Only one of the three natural arches sticking up from the ocean remains, but it's uber-photogenic. Plus, the beach is an excellent vantage point for viewing marine mammals offshore and shorebirds in the adjoining wetlands. Sea life abounds in the tide pools, and the park's **Monarch Grove** draws Monarch butterflies each Spring.

West Cliff Drive and Swanton Boulevard
831-423-4609
www.parks.ca.gov/?page_id=541

Museum: Santa Cruz Surfing Museum

Surfer dudes and anyone interested in surfing history will love this rad little museum, housed in the historic **Mark Abbott Memorial Lighthouse** atop a promontory overlooking world-famous **Steamer Lane** point break, ridden by experts. To make a half day of things, incorporate it into a walk along West Cliff Drive.

Mark Abbott Lighthouse
701 West Cliff Drive
831-420-6289
www.cityofsantacruz.com

Outdoors: Año Nuevo State Park

Few other places in the world let you get so close to elephant seals and with so much ease. Simply park the car and follow the boardwalk alongside the beach, where annually thousands of these marine mammals return to mate and give birth, with the huge males battling it out.

1 New Years Creek Road, Pescadero
650-879-2025
www.parks.ca.gov/?page_id=523

Venue: Capitola

Five miles south of Santa Cruz, more chicly bohemian Capitola Village by the Sea is a relaxed hillside resort village that flows down to an 855-foot-long wooden pier. Take a stroll, fish from the pier, or rent a kayak at the pier's base for a dolphin-spotting excursion in the bay.

www.capitolavillage.com

Trip Planning

Visitor Information Center
303 Water Street, Suite 100
831-425-1234
www.santacruz.org

SAN JOSE

SAN JOSE IS often thought of as an also-ran compared to neighboring San Francisco. But what California's third-largest city lacks in grandiose physical setting, it more than makes up for in its wealth of stellar attractions— many of them inspired by its stature as the epicenter of high-tech Silicon Valley. San Jose's unmistakable cutting-edge techy-ness awaits exploration at The Tech Interactive ultra-hands-on museum, as well as at both the nearby NASA Ames Research Center and Lick Observatory.

There's history here too. In fact, founded in 1777, San Jose served as California's first capital. Yesteryear buildings speckle the glitzy downtown, and the San Jose Museum of Art spotlights contemporary and modern art. The Rosicrucian Egyptian Museum complex teems with enough ancient relics to give the Smithsonian fits of jealousy. Plus, for the quirky and surreal, don't fail to explore the Winchester Mystery House, beloved by kids, as is the California Great America amusement park.

Rosicrucian Egyptian Museum & Planetarium

1660 Park Avenue • 408-947-3635 • www.egyptianmuseum.org

✓ Move over Smithsonian! The largest collection of Egyptian artifacts on exhibit in North America is displayed at the Rosicrucian Egyptian Museum complex, covering an entire city block downtown. Architecturally inspired by the Temple of Amon at Karnak, this phenomenal venue was created by H. Spencer Lewis, the founder of the mysterious Rosicrucian Order. The *Sekhmet* (lion goddess) statue that once stood on his desk is among more than 4,000 Egyptian, as well as Assyrian and Babylonian, artifacts that will make you go "wow!" Beyond the entrance, you'll find genuine mummies (including one of a child, plus others of a cat, a baboon, and even a fish) and scrolls, as well as cast replicas of King Tutankhamen's golden sarcophagus and the Rosetta stone.

A research library displays ancient first-edition books by such big-name Rosicrucians as Francis Bacon and Isaac Newton. And take time to explore the complex's **Peace Garden** (laid out in Egyptian fashion) and to walk the adjacent **Rosicrucian Labyrinth and Alchemy Garden**. A Moorish-designed planetarium screens such shows as NASA's *The 3D Sun*.

Rosicrucian Egyptian Museum entrance. (Courtesy Rosicrucian Egyptian Museum)

Winchester Mystery House. (Courtesy San Jose CVB)

Winchester Mystery House

525 South Winchester Boulevard • 408-247-2000
www.winchestermysteryhouse.com

✓ You'd swear it must be a stage-set from a horror movie or maybe a Disneyland amusement park venue. But no, this real-life 160-room Victorian mansion was built by Sarah Winchester, heiress to the Winchester Rifle fortune, as her bizarre home. It took 38 years to complete due to her nonstop and seemingly senile—and truly mysterious—additions (she was still building in 1922 when she passed away). One door opens to a 15-foot drop into the garden! Another drops into a kitchen sink. You'll even open others that reveal only walls. Inevitably, there are stairs that go nowhere, and no shortage of secret passages. Legend has it she was inspired to build in such illogical fashion after a psychic told her it would appease the ghosts of those killed by the Winchester rifle!

You can well imagine you've ended up in Narnia after walking through the front door, not least for the closet that, when opened, extends through 30 rooms. Kids will especially love it! Marvels for adults include a surfeit of Tiffany stained-glass windows.

Falafel's Drive-In

2301 Stevens Creek Boulevard • 408-294-7886 • www.falafelsdrivein.com

☑ If you're familiar with the Food Network show *Diners, Drive-Ins and Dives* with Guy Fieri, you'll probably recall seeing Falafel's Drive-In profiled. This fab fave of locals has been a San Jose institution for five decades. "Feeling awful? Have a falafel" is its jovial tagline. One bite into your made-to-order falafel pita, and you're hooked! And what a falafel it is, courtesy of Israeli immigrants Zahie and Anton Nijmeh, who opened this roadside attraction in 1966. The thing to order is the bargain-priced daily special—a real beast of a pita filled to bursting with fresh chopped vegetables, falafel balls, and creamy tahini sauce. Bonus: it comes with a fresh banana shake.

You can also choose other authentic Middle Eastern dishes, as well as such drive-in classics as cheeseburgers, juicy burritos, and even hot dogs. Regardless, embrace the mess! At the very least, you have to try the delicious fried chickpea balls made with a perfect blend of fresh herbs and spices. Savor your still-hot falafel family style at the drive-in's shaded patio with classic drive-in bench seating.

Falafel's Drive-In. (Copyright and credit Ramar Lumière Photography)

Nearby Alternatives

Venue: NASA Ames Research Center

Want to check out a *real* Moon rock? Or maybe you're curious how astronauts live and work in space. Then head to NASA's Ames Research Center, where you can even explore inside a mock space station and enjoy a flight simulation through the Milky Way in the IMAX theater.
Moffett Field, Mountain View
650-604-5000
www.nasa.gov/ames

Venue: Lick Observatory

A one-hour serpentine drive to the summit of Hamilton Mountain delivers you to the Lick Observatory, which has been at the forefront of astronomical research since 1888. You'll marvel at its giant telescopes and their mind-blowing discoveries, as well as the stunning views over San Jose below. The observatory is open Thursday–Sunday afternoons.
7281 Mt. Hamilton Road, Mt. Hamilton
408-274-5061
www.ucobservatories.org/observatory/lick-observatory/

Activity: California's Great America

Silicon Valley's high-tech gets wed to state-of-the-art thrill rides at this long-time family-favorite amusement-and-water park, featuring the **Pacific Surge** waterslide. Adrenalin-junkies can scream their lungs out on **Gold Striker**, one of the tallest and fastest roller coasters in California. Youngsters can whoop it up with relatively low-key rides in **Planet Snoopy**.
4701 Great America Parkway
408-988-1776
www.cagreatamerica.com

Museum: The Tech Interactive

This family-friendly science and technology center for wannabe boffins surely ranks as one of the most innovative places on earth. Teeming with experimental science labs, hands-on activities, and design-challenge experiences, it sparks curiosity and creativity in equal measure, regardless of age. An interactive IMAX dome theater raises the "wow!" factor.
201 South Market Street
408-294-8324
www.thetech.org

Trip Planning

San Jose Convention & Visitors Bureau

408 Almaden Boulevard
408-792-4511
www.sanjose.org

SAN FRANCISCO

SAN FRANCISCO IS just plain darn cool! And we're not talking about the often-foggy weather. Boasting the most jaw-dropping bayside setting in North America, it's also chock-full of awesome things to see and do. Nonetheless, from walking the iconic Golden Gate Bridge to exploring among the pagodas and markets of Chinatown, some things stand out as the cream of the crop simply because they're so quintessentially San Franciscan.

First, there's the cable cars, and then the arcing waterfront with world-famous Fisherman's Wharf and its sea lions and steaming outdoor cauldrons of fresh-caught Dungeness crab. And let's not forget Golden Gate Park, boasting two of the city's finest museums, plus botanic gardens and so much more. Speaking of museums: art lovers rave over the Museum of Modern Art and the Legion of Honor. Plus, San Francisco is acknowledged as the epicurean epicenter of the West Coast, with every ethnic cuisine under the sun.

The Waterfront

* Pier 39, The Embarcadero & Beach Street • 415-981-7437 • www.pier39.com
* Fisherman's Wharf, The Embarcadero & Pier 47
  415-674-7503 • www.fishermanswharf.org
* San Francisco Maritime National Historic Park, Jefferson Street
  & Hyde Street • 415-561-7000 • www.nps.gov/safr/index.htm

✓ A stroll along the San Francisco shoreline is a delight, with its squawking seagulls and briny air. The two-mile walk from the Ferry Building to Hyde Street Pier combines spectacular bay vistas with distinct waterfront neighborhoods and blockbuster sights.

Today a foodie mecca, the **Ferry Building** is a great place to pick up a picnic lunch before setting out. Interpretive plaques provide historical context as you walk north past the wharfs, such as at **Pier 1**, where the *San Francisco Belle* paddle wheeler docks. The next highlight is the **Exploratorium**—a superb hands-on science museum at Pier 15. Half-day cruise-tours to Alcatraz Island depart from **Pier 33**. Barking sea lions lure you on to touristy **Pier 39**, with its amusement arcades, souvenir stores, and carousel.

A few blocks farther north, at Pier 47, kitschy, overpriced **Fisherman's Wharf** still has a few working fishing boats worth perusing. Now let the towering masts ahead guide you to **Hyde Street Pier** and its collection of restored historic ships. Finally, head up Hyde to the cable car turnaround and grab a ride.

The waterfront and Golden Gate Bridge.
(Credit Umer Sayyam; courtesy San Francisco Travel Authority)

Golden Gate Park

501 Stanyon Street • 415-831-2700 • goldengatepark.com

☑ Consider an entire day to explore this iconic—and massive (1,017 acres, and 3 miles long)—park, with its equally oversize choice of museums, gardens, and activities. Download a map from the website, and plan out your preferred sites and mode of locomotion. The big five not-to-miss destinations are the California Academy of Sciences, the de Young Museum, the Japanese Tea Garden, the San Francisco Botanical Garden, and the Conservatory of Flowers. They cluster near the park's eastern end.

Golden Gate Park, California Academy of Sciences. (Courtesy San Francisco Travel Authority)

The **California Academy of Sciences** alone could hold you spellbound for hours with its phenomenal aquarium, planetarium, and natural history museum. Now stroll a stone's throw to the **de Young**, showcasing an extraordinary collection of American art spanning four centuries. Break for a cuppa in the **Japanese Tea Garden**, with its pagodas and teahouse. To its south, the **San Francisco Botanical Garden** lets you stroll metaphorically through an Andean cloud forest and other geographical distinct gardens. Finally, explore the astounding **Conservatory of Flowers**: a San Francisco landmark since 1879, the giant glass hothouse is a veritable floral *Fantasia*.

The Waterfront Restaurant

Pier 7, The Embarcadero • 415-391-2696 • www.waterfrontsf.com

✓ A perk of visiting San Francisco is being able to dine with a killer water view. You're spoiled for choice, but the low-lit, contemporary-styled Waterfront Restaurant with soaring wood-beamed ceiling enjoys one of the most sweeping vistas of the Bay Bridge, *San Francisco Belle* stern-wheeler, and Berkeley Hills. The uber-attentive waiters wear vests and black ties (that's San Francisco), but the mood is casual elegant. On warm days (and nights), choose the cozy open-air patio.

This five-decades-old institution is renowned for its deliciously fresh, sustainable seafood. The combo of fine-dining fare and sublime setting explains why it's A-list menu of patrons spans Hunter S. Thompson and Lady Gaga to Bill Clinton and Barack Obama. You can't go wrong with its Dungeness crab cakes, classic cioppino, lobster risotto, and Whole Wood Oven-Roasted Dungeness Crab with Handmade Linguini. The American-fare menu also includes bacon-wrapped chicken breast, plus juicy filet of beef tenderloin with fingerling potatoes, spinach, and Bordelaise sauce. It even has vegan dishes. Save room for some sticky toffee pudding or a classic creme brûlée.

The Waterfront Restaurant patio. (Courtesy The Waterfront Restaurant)

Nearby Alternatives

Museum: Legion of Honor

With its breathtaking setting overlooking the Pacific and the Golden Gate Bridge, the beautiful beaux-arts Legion of Honor displays an astounding collection comprising 124,000 works of European art spanning 4,000 years, from ancient Egyptian to Rubens, Renoir, and Rembrandt. Its many sculptures by Rodin include *The Thinker*—the museum's emblem.

100 34th Avenue
415-750-3600
legionofhonor.famsf.org

Venue: Chinatown

From the iconic Dragon Gate to its dim sum restaurants, San Francisco's densely packed, bustling Chinatown is a true slice of China transplanted. You'll easily fill an afternoon here wandering its vibrant markets and colorful alleyways. Don't miss the **Chinese Cultural Center** and the two-story **China Live** marketplace and food emporium.

843 Grant Avenue
888-212-3203
www.sanfranciscochinatown.com

Activity: Walk the Golden Gate Bridge

Don warm clothing—especially in foggy summer—for the 1.5-mile walk across the world's most famous bridge. A scything cold wind is often blowing, but the views of the city, Alcatraz, and the bay are stupendous. Start at the **Bridge Welcome Center** (on the southeast), with its fascinating interpretative exhibits.

Golden Gate Bridge
Visitor Plaza
Lincoln Boulevard at I-101
415-921-5858
www.goldengate.org

Museum: Museum of Modern Art (MOMA)

Nirvana for those who appreciate contemporary and modern art, MOMA recently emerged from a major expansion that tripled its exhibition space. Its more than 33,000 works tick off an A-list of names: Frida Kahlo, Jackson Pollock, Richard Serra, Georgia O'Keeffe. This downtown delight might hold you in its spell the entire day.

151 Third Street
415-357-4000
www.sfmoma.org

Trip Planning

Visitor Information Bureau

749 Howard Street
415-391-2000
www.sftravel.com

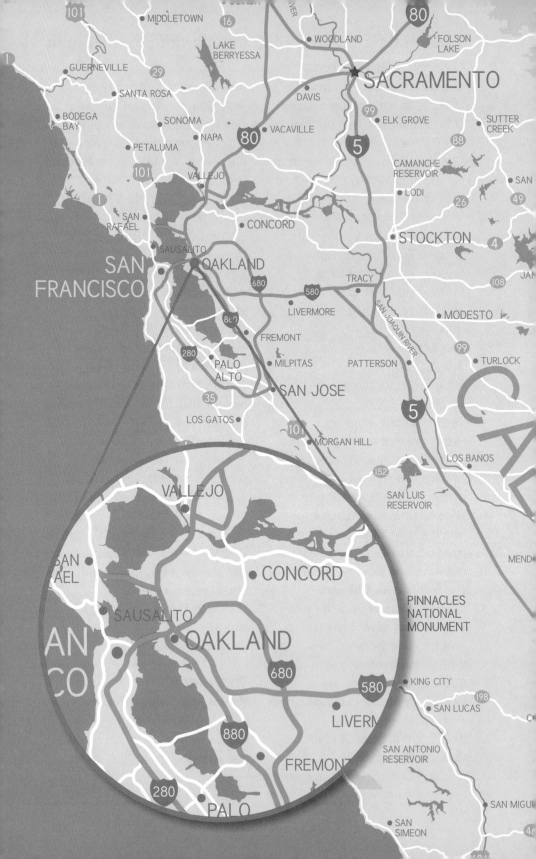

EAST BAY

{ Oakland & Berkeley }

SAN FRANCISCO'S *OTHER* BRIDGE—the Bay Bridge—connects "The City" to the East Bay cities of Oakland and Berkeley, whose bragging rights include a world-class university, a famously liberal multiethnic culture, a sunny Mediterranean climate, and Alice Waters's groundbreaking Chez Panisse restaurant. Good luck securing a reservation at the birthplace of "farm to table" California nouvelle cuisine! No worries: the East Bay boasts scores of world-class restaurants, plus a roster of tremendous live music venues.

The UC Berkeley campus is only the tip of the iceberg representing the East Bay's free-spirited and avant-garde culture. Stroll Telegraph Avenue, with its legendary bookstores. Walk or cycle the Bay Trail around the Jack London Square waterfront. Check out the arts and history scene at the Oakland Museum of California, or hike in the hilltop forests at Reinhart Redwood Regional Park. The Lawrence Livermore Hall of Science and Oakland Zoo will delight the kids too.

University of California at Berkeley Campus

UC Berkeley Koret Visitor Center • 210 Stadium Rim Way
510-642-5215 • www.berkeley.edu

☑ "Berkeley" is synonymous with the University of California (UC)—or "Cal"—and a history of liberal student activism. The town wouldn't be the same without the sylvan and storied heart-of-the-city campus, with its grandiose buildings and redwood groves. Much more than a mere academic enclave, the 178-acre landscaped campus is open to the public—a fantastic destination in its own right.

The **Koret Visitor Center**, in California Memorial Stadium, offers views over the campus. From here, a counterclockwise loop should take in the 307-feet-tall **Campanile** (aka Sather Tower), with its observation deck offering a spectacular 360-degree vista of the Bay Area. Don't miss both the **Bancroft Library** and **Moffett Library**—architectural treasures of the UC system for their grandiose marble interiors and vaulted ceilings. Continue west via the **Eucalyptus Grove** to explore the new **Berkeley Art Museum**. Then retrace your steps east via redwood-shaded **Strawberry Creek** to **Sproul Plaza**, Cal's famous hub of demonstrations since birthing the 1964 Free Speech Movement. Finally, pass under Sather Gate to stroll **Telegraph Avenue**—the epicenter of the tumultuous 1960s counterculture scene.

University of California Berkeley campus,
Berkeley Art Museum. (Courtesy Visit Berkeley)

Oakland Museum of California. (Courtesy of Oakland Museum of California)

Oakland Museum of California (OMCA)

1000 Oak Street, Oakland • 510-318-8400 • www.museumca.org

✓ Want the lowdown on local history? Want to put your East Bay experiences in cultural perspective? Then indulge in a few hours perusing this sensational regional museum and long-time East Bay cultural institution specializing in the art, history, and natural sciences of California—past, present, and future. In recent years, it's focused more keenly on untold narratives and quirky groundbreaking exhibits, such as of spectacular art installations from the annual Burning Man festival. OMCA's interactive exhibits draw on first-person accounts by people who have shaped California's cultural heritage. Dorothea Lange's photography of people in desperate circumstances is a highlight, as are permanent exhibits on Native American peoples, the gold rush of 1849, and the Black Power movement.

With 1.9 million objects in its collection and a sprawling seven-acre campus that includes beautiful terraced gardens with views of Lake Merritt, there's a lot to cover. Besides its fascinating galleries, OMCA has regular education programs and community events, such as drop-in art workshops, plus Friday Nights @ OMCA outdoor parties with gourmet food trucks and live music.

Zachary's Chicago Pizza

5801 College Avenue, Oakland • 510-655-6385 • www.zacharys.com

✔ The Bay Area's reigning mecca of pizza since it opened its original restaurant in Oakland's Rockridge district in 1983, Zachary's Chicago Pizza has exploded in popularity and now boasts five East Bay locations. When founders Zach Zachowski and Barbara Gabel retired in 2003, they sold the business to their employees. Zach's still has diners lining up outside the door to savor the pizzeria's scrumptious, Windy City–inspired deep-dish pizzas featuring a signature flaky, golden-brown buttery crust. The wait is well worth it, although you can call ahead and order a "half-baked" pizza to go.

There's a reason Zach's has won every popularity poll you can think of. Their "stuffed" pizza, with fillings between two thin-crust dough layers and smothered with zesty, diced tomato sauce, are the main draw, best savored accompanied by a fresh salad and hearty wine. Of course, it also serves traditional pizzas, made to order with whatever fresh ingredients you choose. The 100 percent employee-owned pizza joint is family friendly. Plus, check out the walls displaying pizza art created by patrons spanning four decades.

Zachary's pizza.
(Courtesy Zachary's
Chicago Pizza)

Nearby Alternatives

Venue: Oakland Zoo

This world-class zoo in the Oakland Hills is home to more than 700 native and exotic animals, grouped by geographic area or ecosystem. Watch elephants chill in their splashing pond or gibbons leaping in a tropical rainforest. Youngsters get their own section with a train carousel and one-on-one Animal Encounters.
9777 Golf Links Road, Oakland
510-632-9525
www.oaklandzoo.org

Outdoors: Reinhart Redwood Regional Park

Take your pick of half a dozen contiguous regional parks that cap the Berkeley and Oakland Hills. The miles of trails lacing Reinhart Redwood Regional Park lead into a hidden, peaceful grove of stately 150-foot-tall coast redwood trees—rare survivors of 19th-century logging. With luck, you may spot deer and golden eagles.
7867 Redwood Road, Oakland
510-544-3127
www.ebparks.org/parks/ redwood

Venue: Jack London Square

Even San Francisco struggles to compete with Jack London Square for its combo of Bay views, shorefront esplanade and recreational trail, a booming bar and restaurant scene, plus such historic attractions as **Heinold's First and Last Saloon**, **Jack London's Yukon Cabin**, President Roosevelt's **USS *Potomac***, and a decommissioned floating lighthouse-turned-museum.
Embarcadero West and Broadway
www.baytrail.org
www.jacklondonsquare.com

Museum: Lawrence Hall of Science

High in the Berkeley Hills, this science hall abounds with fun educational and interactive exhibits for visitors of all ages, from planetarium shows to live animal encounters. It's named for Ernest Lawrence, Nobel Prize-winning inventor of the cyclotron particle accelerator at UC Berkeley's Lawrence Laboratory, in the building below. It has stupendous bay views.
1 Centennial Drive, Berkeley
510-642-5132
www.lawrencehallofscience.org

Trip Planning

2030 Addison Street, Berkeley
510-549-7040
www.visitberkeley.com
481 Water Street, Oakland
510-839-9000
www.visitoakland.com

SAUSALITO

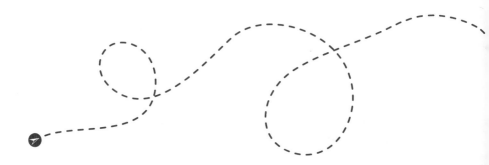

I'S HARD TO imagine that this laid-back and distinctly wealthy and artsy Mediterranean-style Bayshore town was a major shipbuilding center in World War II. A bucket-list destination for any traveler to Northern California, the picturesque seaside town to the northern side of the Golden Gate Bridge is renowned for its killer view across the bay to San Francisco, as well as for its houseboat community spanning millionaire homes to funky "Popeye" creations.

With fab restaurants and shopping, the town is also superbly positioned for explorations to nearby attractions that should also be on sage travelers' bucket lists: Muir Woods National Monument for redwood groves; the Marin Headlands for unsurpassed vistas; World War II batteries; the Marina Mammal Center; Angel Island, the headland's water-girt "twin" perfect for hiking; and Stinson Beach for sunning, surfing, fishing, and more. No wonder San Francisco's bon vivants choose to get away here on the ferry on weekends.

Walking Tour

Sausalito Ice House Visitors Center & Museum
780 Bridgeway • 415-332-0505 • www.sausalitohistoricalsociety.com

☑ A walk the length of the Sausalito waterfront, from the kid-focused **Bay Area Discovery Museum** (*www.bayareadiscoverymuseum.org*) at the foot of the Golden Gate Bridge to the houseboats at Waldo Point Harbor, is a relaxing, fun way to explore. If the full four-mile walk seems too long, skip the museum or simply concentrate on the short downtown walking tour suggested by the Sausalito Historical Society: begin at the society's **Ice House Visitor Center and Museum**, a stone's throw from the Golden Gate ferry terminal. The route is lined with interpretative historical plaques.

Returning to the Visitor Center, continue west along Bridgeway. The entire route is lined by wharves where yachts bob at anchor. First of the must-stops is **Studio 333**, a local artist cooperative gallery (turn left at Locust Street, then right on Caledonia Street). Continue on Bridgeway past Sausalito Yacht Harbor to the **Bay Model Visitor Center** (administered by the US Army Corps of Engineers), displaying a 1.5-acre working hydraulic model of the San Francisco Bay. Finally, a half-mile along, you'll arrive at **Waldo Point Harbor**, where some 500 eclectic houseboats are a sight to behold!

Sausalito walking tour, Sausalito. (Credit Kyle Hawton, CC BY-SA 3.0, via Wikimedia Commons)

Muir Woods National Monument

1 Muir Woods Road • 415-388-2595
www.nps.gov/muwo

☑ Tucked into an isolated, ocean-facing canyon of Mount
Tamalpais, this glorious stand of old-growth coast
redwoods was named for conservationist John Muir, who
inspired President Teddy Roosevelt to protect it in 1908.
Strolling through the dank and dark cathedral, with its
nave of 1,000-year-old giants that soar 250 feet, induces a
profound sense of awe.

Flat, easy trails with raised boardwalks loop through the
groves and include interpretive displays. In the light gaps
beneath the redwoods, you'll spot California big leaf maples,
Douglas fir, red alders, and tanoaks, as well as ferns, redwood
sorrel, and fallen redwoods smothered in fungi littering the
forest floor. This shrine to Mother Nature also abounds with
wildlife, including deer, raccoons, skunks, and even river
otters in Redwood Creek! And, of course, there's no shortage
of birdlife, from owls to woodpeckers and Pacific wrens.

Parking lots fill up early in summer and on weekends.
Arrive first thing in the morning if you want to enjoy the
solitude at its most pristine. Check the website for guided
bird-watching, nature walks, and other interpretive programs.

Muir Woods National Monument. (Copyright Sarbjit Bahga,
CC BY-SA 4.0, via Wikimedia Commons)

The Trident

558 Bridgeway • 415-331-3232
www.thetrident.net

☑ Perched on the Sausalito waterfront with a knockout view of San Francisco and the Bay, this prime seaside real estate has history as long as your arm. The turn-of-the-century landmark built in 1898 housed the San Francisco Yacht Club, later became a jazz club, and morphed into an infamous bar-restaurant-music venue with psychedelic murals in 1966. Today a classy seafood restaurant, the sixties decor—featuring rich woodwork and curved booths—is still there to admire. Plus, an onstage jazz trio adds a touch of yesteryear cool.

The mouthwatering menu begins with such spicy starters as a Dungeness crab kimchi "martini," oysters with "hogwash," and a jumbo prawn cocktail with an explosive dollop of horseradish or a choice of milder tartar sauce. Or maybe you'd prefer fried calamari stacked on a boat-shaped plate and topped with shreds of seaweed, daikon, and peppers. Salads? Check out the Bibb & Blu: beet with burrata. Entrées? Take your pick from fish 'n' chips to seafood linguini, or the signature house cioppino. On weekends, head to the upstairs deck for brunch.

The Trident, Sausalito. (Courtesy The Trident)

Nearby Alternatives

Drive: Marin Headlands

Begin your clockwise loop drive of this rugged wilderness on Conzelman Road, with a spectacular view of the Golden Gate Bridge and San Francisco. Hike the trail to **Point Bonita**. Check out the World War II batteries and Nike Missile Site. Then drop down to Rodeo Beach and its **Marine Mammal Center** (*www.marinemammalcenter.org*). 948 Fort Barry 415-331-1540 or 415-561-4700 www.nps.gov/goga/marin-headlands.htm www.parksconservancy.org/parks/marin-headlands

Outdoors: Stinson Beach

This gorgeous white-sand beach arcs for three miles around Bolinas Bay. On hot days and weekends, it draws visitors for hiking, picnicking, surfing, and fishing—simply cast a line from the beach. The quiet, woodsy beach community behind the beach has three casual restaurants. Golden Gate National Recreation Area Building 201, Fort Mason 415-561-4700 www.nps.gov/goga/stbe.htm

Outdoors: Angel Island State Park

This sylvan, history-rich island in San Francisco Bay makes for a perfect half-day escape via ferry from Tiburon or San Francisco. Trails lead up Mount Livermore for breathtaking 360-degree views. The island served as an immigration center, World War II prison, and Nike missile base. Don't miss the **Angel Island Immigration Museum** (closed Monday and Tuesday). Ayala Cove Information Kiosk Ayala Cove, Angel Island 415-435-5390 or 415-435-1915 www.angelisland.com www.aiisf.org

Venue: Tiburon

This beautiful Mediterranean-style town with unobstructed views of the San Francisco skyline was once a major maritime and railroad town. Catch up on that history at the **Railroad & Ferry Depot Museum**, then stroll the waterfront, and maybe go paddleboarding or kayaking before hopping a ferry to Angel Island. Destination Tiburon 1505 Tiburon Boulevard 415-435-2298 www.destinationtiburon.org

Trip Planning

Sausalito Chamber of Commerce 1913 Bridgeway • 415-331-7262 www.visitsausalito.org

SANTA ROSA

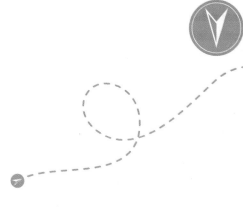

ONLY 55 MILES north of San Francisco, Santa Rosa makes a great base for exploring the Sonoma and Russian River regions. But this charming and peaceful city is a fabulous destination in its own right, despite being overlooked by visitors hurrying to explore the surrounding wine country.

The Santa Rosa Visitor Center, in the old railroad depot in Santa Rosa's Historic Railroad Square, is the logical starting point. This lovely neighborhood is replete with antique stores, coffee houses, specialty shops, and gourmet restaurants. Fans of Snoopy and the *Peanuts* cartoon should prioritize a visit to the Charles M. Schulz Museum. Botanical aficionados will enjoy the Luther Burbank Home & Garden, and aviation buffs must see the Pacific Coast Air Museum.

Nonetheless, Santa Rosa is one destination where the two top recommended sites and experiences—the Russian River wineries and Armstrong Redwoods State Park—are close together outside town for a perfect combo.

Russian River Wineries

Russian River Valley Winegrowers • P.O. Box 16, Fulton • 707-521-2534
www.russianrivervalley.org/wineries

✓ The Russian River Valley northwest of Santa Rosa is renowned as the epicenter of the appellation that set the standard for cool-climate California Pinot Noir and Chardonnay grapes. Extending over 15,000 vineyard acres, it lures visitors to enjoy scenic drives along Highway 116 (the "Gravenstein Highway") between Sebastopol and Forestville, and River Road between Fulton and Guerneville. Top wineries line each route, and most welcome visitors. Many are known for growing Gewürztraminer, Pinot Gris, and even cool-climate Syrah. This American Viticultural Area (AVA) is influenced above all by cool fogs that intrude along the Russian River to the west. Bring a warm jacket, even in summer!

De rigueur stops along the Gravenstein Highway include **Emeritus Vineyards** (*www.emeritusvineyards.com*), with a tasting room offering vistas inside the working winery; legendary **Mom's Apple Pie** shop (*www.momsapplepieusa.com*), a reminder of when this area was given to apples, not vines; and **Russian River Vineyards** (*www.russianrivervineyards.com*)—voted "Best Tasting Room" by the *Santa Rosa Press Democrat*. River Road stops include **Kendall-Jackson's** (*www.kj.com*) chateau and gardens, and the iconic ivy-clad **Korbel Champagne Cellars** (*www.korbel.com*).

Kendall-Jackson Winery. (Courtesy Kendall-Jackson)

Armstrong
Redwoods State Park.
(Courtesy Visit California)

Armstrong Redwoods State Natural Reserve

17000 Armstrong Woods Road • 707-869-2015
www.parks.ca.gov/?page_id=450 • www.russianriver.com

☑ It's an awe-inspiring and humbling experience to walk or, better yet, camp beneath giant coast redwoods—the tallest living trees on our planet! It's impossible to not feel transformed, albeit briefly, by a visit to the Armstrong Redwoods State Natural Reserve, two miles north of the Russian River resort town of **Guerneville**. Spanning 805 acres, this grove of *Sequoia sempervirens* is a rare remnant of the primeval redwood forest that covered much of this region before the logging boom of the late 19th century.

Start at the visitor center near the entrance. From here, almost 10 miles of self-guided nature trails meander through this silent sylvan retreat, whose oldest tree—**Colonel Armstrong**—is more than 1,400 years old. Its tallest—**Parson Jones**—soars skyward for more than 310 feet . . . taller than a football field is long! These trees are so tall that the tops are often lost to view in the mists that help sustain this temperate rainforest. Horseback rides are offered. The forest was badly damaged by fire in August 2020. Check the park website for updates.

Ca'Bianca

835 Second Street • 707-542-5800
www.cabianca.com

☑ A lovely white Victorian clapperboard mansion provides a perfectly romantic setting for one of the best Italian restaurants in Northern California. Some three decades ago, husband and wife Marco Diana and Karin Hoehne restored the historic Marshall House as an elegant restaurant, with crystal chandeliers, carved ceiling moldings, and subtle frescoes. Lovely! Or opt for the shaded wraparound veranda or leafy outdoor patio dining, with heat lamps in winter.

The menu spans the length of Italy, from Milan in the north to Messina, in Sicily, using fresh local, organic ingredients and house-made bread and pasta made daily. Start perhaps with a delicious garden-fresh salad; clams and mussels sautéed with leeks, garlic, and white wine; or perhaps baked layers of eggplant, tomato, and mozzarella. Scrumptious entrées include gnocchetti with porcini; pork tenderloin topped with pears and Gorgonzola simmered in a port wine reduction; and ravioli stuffed with salmon and zucchini draped with rich and creamy mascarpone sauce. Leave room for the chocolate terrine. Wash it all down with a hearty wine!

Ca'Bianca entrée. (Courtesy Ca'Bianca)

Nearby Alternatives

Venue: Luther Burbank Home & Garden

It was here that renowned horticulturist Luther Burbank (1849-1926)—the "Wizard of Horticulture"—lived and experimented with plant breeding for most of his 50-year career. His Greek-revival home is furnished as if he still lived there. And the gardens are planted with Shasta daisies, Burbank potatoes, plums, and other Burbank creations.

204 Santa Rosa Avenue
707-524-5445
www.lutherburbank.org

Venue: Railroad Square Historic District

Santa Rosa's historic "Old Town" is listed on the National Register of Historic Places and covers 14 square blocks to either side of the old railroad, centered on Railroad Square. Step back in time as you explore its beautifully restored buildings hosting antique stores, boutiques, restaurants, and wine cellars.

9 Fourth Street
707-542-5306
www.railroadsquare.net

Museum: Charles M. Schulz Museum

For 50 years, Santa Rosa resident Charles "Sparky" Schulz drew the *Peanuts* comic strip, with Charlie Brown and Snoopy the beagle. This museum brings it all to life with a re-creation of Schulz's studio, his original comic art, *Peanuts* movie screenings, and even a Snoopy's-head labyrinth in the outdoor gardens.

2301 Hardies Lane
707-579-4452
www.schulzmuseum.org

Museum: Pacific Coast Air Museum

If military history and aviation are your bag, you'll thrill to this superb museum at the Charles M. Schulz Airport. The almost 40 beautifully preserved historic aircraft displayed include such icons as a F-4 Phantom, F-14 Tomcat, a Harrier jump jet, and a Vietnam-era Huey helicopter. Many of the aircraft are still airworthy.

1 Air Museum Way
707-575-7900
www.pacificcoastairmuseum.org

Trip Planning

9 Fourth Street
707-577-8674
www.visitsantarosa.com

NAPA VALLEY

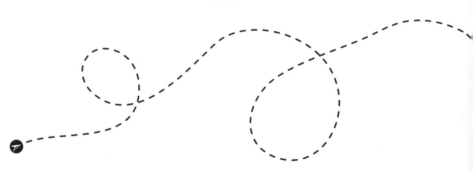

EVERYONE, SURELY, KNOWS Napa Valley as ground zero for North America's premier wines. Dotted with more than 400 wineries, and the first officially designated AVA in the United States, this narrow and elongated valley is home to many of the most hallowed wineries and restaurants in the country. Visits to venerable vineyards and boutique estates for a guided tour and to sip award-winning wines is reason enough for a beeline. But don't fail to make the most of the intoxicating natural setting. Bicycle the Silverado Trail along the valley's lesser traveled east side. Kayak the River Napa, or let a gondolier punt you. Maybe savor a spa treatment at a lavish resort or in one of Calistoga's world-famous thermal mud baths.

Then there's the Wine Train, an early hot-air balloon ride, golfing, and, of course, gourmet dining at Michelin-starred restaurants that are highlights of Napa, Yountville, and St. Helena.

Downtown Napa

Napa Downtown Association • 1290 First Street • 707-257-322
www.donapa.com • www.napar600riverfront.com

✓ Most first-time visitors to Napa Valley hustle past the gateway town, eager to get to the wineries. Yet the largest of the valley's towns has a history-laden downtown with heaps to hold your attention, from a fab farmers market to a cool riverside walk. The river that bisects the leafy city also birthed it in the 1840s as a trade and transportation hub. Napa's lovely Victorian mansions today house celebrity-led restaurants, boutique shops, classy B&Bs, and, of course, lots of hip wine bars, thanks to a recent restoration and renaissance highlighted by construction of the **Napa River Promenade**.

Stroll the beautiful promenade alongside the meandering river, noting the historical plaques and old mill buildings now repurposed as fashionable restaurants and more. Then consider a romantic exploration of the river with **Napa Valley Gondola** (*www.napavalleygondola.com*), or rent kayaks and paddle yourself. Keep your eye out for beavers! Next, explore **Oxbow Market**, a lively 40,000-square-foot gourmet food hall. And downtown is replete with fabulous public art: grab a map from the visitor center to guide you.

Downtown Napa, Riverwalk. (Credit Bob McClenahan; courtesy Visit Napa Valley)

Calistoga

Calistoga Welcome Center • 1133 Washington Street
707-942-6333 • www.visitcalistoga.com

✓ At the narrow northern end of Napa Valley, this cute little spa town lined with early 1900s buildings is world-renowned for its geothermal hot spring pools and mud baths. There are other reasons to visit, but the many hot springs resorts are the "Spa Capital of Northern California's" top draw. Don't leave without experiencing the quintessential mud bath treatment at **Dr. Wilkinson's Hot Springs Resort** (*www.drwilkinson. com*). And don't miss **Old Faithful Geyser**, a smaller (yet still impressive) equal to Yellowstone's, erupting every 15 to 30 minutes.

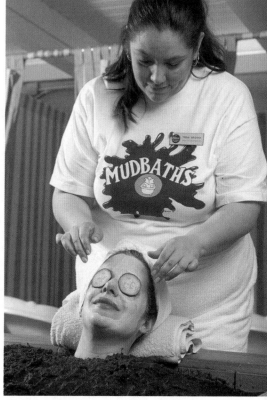

Calistoga, Dr Wilkinson's Spa mud bath. (Courtesy Wilkinson's Spa)

Stellar wineries hereabouts include attention-grabbing hilltop **Sterling Vineyards** (*www.sterlingvineyards.com*), accessed via a funicular railway; and, below, the medieval-style, multi-turreted **Castello di Amorosa** (*www.castellodiamorosa.com*), with its frescoed great hall and even a torture chamber ("So, you don't like our wines?"), like a set from *Game of Thrones* transplanted! In town, simply strolling downtown Lincoln Avenue is a joy: it's lined with quaint shops, art galleries, and haute cuisine restaurants. Kids in tow? Then head to the **Petrified Forest** and to **Safari West** (*www.safariwest.com*): a 400-acre wildlife preserve, explored on a mini-safari by Jeep.

Mustards Grill

7399 St. Helena Highway, Napa • 707-944-2424 • www.mustardsgrill.com

✓ We know you'd give your right arm to dine at the near-impossible-to-reserve French Laundry. But the iconic Mustards Grill roadhouse is also one of Napa Valley's most satisfying and original restaurants. Arrive in spring, and you'll find the surrounding vineyards ablaze with bright yellow wild mustard flowers.

Owner-chef Cindy Pawlcyn is a wine country pioneer and an instructor at the nearby Culinary Institute of America. So, you can expect fab fare, and perhaps a wait to be seated, giving you the chance to stroll the on-site bountiful gardens from which much of the kitchen's fresh seasonal greens and veggies are culled.

The innovative menu blends California nouvelle sophistication with heaped plates of honest American fare. For starters, perhaps you'll choose crispy calamari with curried slaw or warm Cabécou goat cheese. Next up might be the grilled halibut sauced with oxtail reduction and served with perfectly cooked silken leeks and fingerling potatoes, or even chipotle-rubbed quail with a wild mushroom tamale, prepared in the wood-burning oven. For dessert, make it the lemon-lime tart capped with brown-sugar meringue.

Mustards Grill dessert. (Courtesy Mustards Grill)

Nearby Alternatives

Venue: The Hess Collection

The stand-apart winery when it comes to art in wine country, this winery's "museum" collection has been hailed as among the world's top 200 galleries. Housed in a historic greystone that's been producing wines since 1903, it's a remarkable visit, which is made more appealing by the award-winning Hess Collections wines.

4411 Redwood Road
707-255-1144
www.hesscollection.com

Venue: Culinary Institute of America (CIA)

The historic landmark greystone building rising over Highway 128 in St. Helena was for many years the Christian Brothers Winery. Today it serves as the CIA at Greystone—one of the world's premier schools for culinary and wine education. Memorable visits include options for a tour or a cooking class.

2555 Main Street, St. Helena
707-967-1100
www.ciachef.edu/cia-california

Activity: Napa Valley Wine Train

There's nothing like sipping a glass of wine in vintage splendor as you gaze upon Napa's gorgeous landscapes rolling by. You'll ride in luxuriously refurbished centenary railcars on a 36-mile round trip, stopping at celebrated Napa Valley wineries en route. Plus, you get to enjoy a gourmet dining experience along the way!

1275 Mckinstry Street, Napa
707-253-2111 or 800-427-4124
www.winetrain.com

Activity: Bicycle the Silverado Trail

With miles of winding country roads, Napa Valley offers a world-class cycling experience, and there's none better than the legendary Silverado Trail. Running along the east side of the valley from Napa to Calistoga for 27 miles, this gently rolling, sublimely scenic, and relatively untrafficked route takes you past a huge selection of wineries.

Napa Valley Bike Tours
950 Pearl South, Napa
707-251-8687
www.napavalleybiketours.com

Trip Planning

1300 First Street, Suite 303, Napa
707-251-5895
www.visitnapavalley.com

SONOMA

RRESISTIBLY CHARMING SONOMA is laden with history. The town—located midway between Santa Rosa and Napa— was headquarters of the Mexican military, and it was here in 1846 that the Bear Flag Revolt of 1846 sparked California's independence. Its 19th-century adobe buildings—including Mission San Francisco Solano and the Sonoma Barracks— comprise Sonoma State Historic Park, which is one of the most important historic enclaves in California.

Situated at the southern end of the renowned Sonoma Valley wine-making region, the hip gentrified town is today known for its wine bars and gourmet restaurants, as well as being a gateway for adventures throughout the lush 17-mile-long valley. The vale's many microclimates provide a fabulous array of terroirs and wine-tasting experiences. Other activity options abound, from hot-air ballooning and bicycling to bird watching in San Pablo Bay National Wildlife Refuge. Plus, there's novelist Jack London's former home to explore in Jack London State Historic Park in quaint Glen Ellen.

Balloon Ride over the Vineyards

Sonoma Ballooning Adventures • 21870 Eighth Street East, Sonoma
707-819-9223 • www.sonomaballooning.com

✓ Rising, literally, with the sunrise is a special thrill and
inspirational joy as you experience the lush rolling
landscape of Sonoma Valley while floating in a hot-air balloon.
You'll feel like a soaring eagle as you drift over vineyards and lush
pockets of wilderness, and "ooh!" and "aah!" at the panoramic
vistas of the distant Pacific Ocean and perhaps even the San
Francisco Bay. The unmatched views and exhilarating sensation
will take your breath away!

You'll launch just after dawn when the temperatures are at
their coolest and the winds are at their calmest. Although flights
typically last about one hour, budget for as long as a four-hour
commitment due to the many variables involved—including
weather and distance back from the indeterminate landing site.
You are, after all, traveling literally with the wind! That means
complete silence—no, there's no wind rushing past you—except
when the propane burners are fired up to keep the balloon at
a desired elevation. Once back in Sonoma, you'll celebrate by
toasting with a traditional sparkling wine and mimosa.

Ballooning in Sonoma. (Courtesy Sonoma Ballooning)

Sonoma State Historic Park, Sonoma Mission. (Credit Carol M. Highsmith)

Sonoma State Historic Park

20 East Spain Street • 707-938-9560 • www.parks.ca.gov/?page_id=479

☑ The town of Sonoma grew up around the northernmost and last Franciscan mission founded in California and the Mexican military barracks of Pueblo de Sonoma, established in 1835 by General Mariano Guadalupe Vallejo. It was here, in June 1846, that US settlers proclaimed a Republic of California in the Bear Flag Revolt that declared independence from Mexico.

Start your walking tour of Sonoma State Historic Park at the **Bear Flag Monument** that stands in Sonoma Plaza. Most buildings that reflect this early history line the north side of the plaza and one block east. The partially restored, two-story adobe **Barracks** once housed Mexican troops. Here, too, are the **Casa Grande** servant quarters and the **Toscano Hotel**, furnished much as it looked when built in the 1850s. To the east, you'll arrive at **Mission San Francisco Solano**, dating from 1824; restored, it contains exhibits on mission life, plus the Jorgensen watercolors of the 21 California missions. Finally, a 15-minute walk to the northwest of the Plaza brings you to General Vallejo's well-preserved former home, the Gothic-style **Lachryma Montis**.

The Girl & The Fig

110 West Spain Street • 707-938-3634 • www.thegirlandthefig.com

✓ As fitting to the Sonoma vibe as a tailored glove, restaurateur Sondra Bernstein's sophisticated French-style bistro enjoys a perfect spot on the northwest corner of Sonoma Plaza. Make it your first choice for dining in town, and be sure to call ahead for a reservation. It's popular with very good reason!

The cozy restaurant focuses on rustic Provençal-inspired classics with a modern twist using fresh, local, in-season ingredients, including garden vegetables and herbs from its own biodynamic farm. Dishes are bursting with flavor! Bernstein oversees a kitchen that makes its own award-winning charcuterie, *salumi*, and other items.

An ideal pairing is perhaps pastis-scented steamed mussels or a straight-from-heaven duck liver mousse with fig jam and brioche toast. Entrée temptations might include lamb cassoulet, or wild flounder meunière with Yukon potato purée, spinach, and lemon-caper brown butter. Portions are generous. But do leave room for the signature salted fig-and-chocolate pudding trifle. Despite the abundance of local wines, the wine list almost sacrilegiously specializes in a unique Rhone wine list. The memory of your dining experience is sure to linger!

The Girl & the Fig. (Courtesy The Girl & the Fig)

Nearby Alternatives

Venues: Sonoma Valley Wineries
With seven distinct terroirs, the Sonoma Valley AVA has oenophiles salivating. Top destinations to visit include the mission-style **St. Francis Winery**, with a superb food-and-wine pairings; the **Ledson** winery chateau; and **Gloria-Ferrer**, in the rolling Carneros hills, for its sparkling wines.
100 Pythian Road
888-675-9463
www.stfranciswinery.com
7335 Highway 12, Kenwood
707-537-3810
www.ledson.com
23555 Arnold Drive
866-845-6742
www.gloriaferrer.com

Venue: Glen Ellen
The charming village of Glen Ellen, tucked off Highway 12, is a marvelous bucolic escape that novelist Jack London called home. It hosts such boutique wineries as **Benziger**. The **Quarryhill Botanical Garden** is renowned for its temperate-climate Asian plants, and kids will love splashing around at **Morton's Warm Springs** Resort.
www.sonomacounty.com/cities/glen-ellen

Venue: Jack London State Historic Park
Fans of Jack London's novels will appreciate an afternoon exploring this state park that preserves London's cottage residence where he wrote many of his works. Shaded within a redwood grove, "The House of Happy Walls" is now a museum. A trail leads to his grave, bathhouse, and lake.
2400 London Ranch Road, Glen Ellen • 707-938-5216
www.jacklondonpark.com

Outdoors: San Pablo Bay National Wildlife Refuge
Sonoma Creek and Napa River empty into San Pablo, where they form a marshy estuary that's nirvana to wildfowl, shorebirds, and nature lovers. Trails lace the San Pablo Bay National Wildlife Refuge, offering especially good sightings of such migratory birds as the ruddy duck and canvasbacks in winter.
2100 Sears Point Road, Sonoma
707-769-4200
www.fws.gov/refuge/san_pablo_bay

Trip Planning

Sonoma Valley Visitors Bureau
453 First Street East, Sonoma
707-996-1090
www.sonomavalley.com
www.sonoma.com

SACRAMENTO

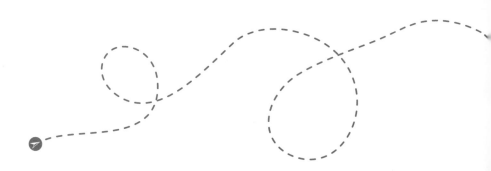

SITUATED IN THE Central Valley, Sacramento rose to prominence during the gold rush era and by 1854 had been named California's capital city. This winsome, laid-back, yet sophisticated city is replete with sites that play up its colorful past, including as terminus of the First Transcontinental Railroad. The superb California State Railroad Museum is one of Sacramento's top draws, enthralling kids from nine to 90 with its collection of 19th-century "iron horses." And the not-to-be-missed state capitol building is open to the public for guided tours; it has an excellent museum and monument-filled park.

The city's other top attractions are all within walking distance, many in the historic downtown, including the Old Sacramento Waterfront District, replete with gold rush–era structures. Nearby, the Crocker Art Museum boasts an impressive collection of California art from the gold rush era. And Sutter's Fort Museum is a restoration of the original adobe buildings that birthed Sacramento.

State Capitol

10th Street & L Street • 916-324-0333
www.capitolmuseum.ca.gov • www.assembly.ca.gov/statecapitol

☑ In the first five years since California became a state in 1850,
its peripatetic capital moved six times! In 1854, the seat of
government settled in Sacramento. Its magnificent, wedding-cake
white neoclassical capitol building—inspired by *the* Capitol in
Washington, DC—was completed in 1874. Take a free docent-led
tour to get the low-down on the building's history and stupendous
architecture, with its gilded Corinthian columns, opulent rotunda,
and murals and statues. If legislators are in session, you can ask to
access the public galleries in the **senate and assembly chambers**
(although not the governor's office).

You'll marvel at the hallway leading to the **Capitol Museum**: It
has 58 dioramas representing each of California's counties.
The museum displays changing exhibits and historical rooms that
offer a view into California's political past. Next, stroll the adjacent
40-acre **Capitol Park**, with its International World Peace Rose
Garden; Civil War Memorial Grove with trees planted in 1897 from
Civil War battlefields; and more than 150 monuments, including
the bell from the USS *California*, sunk at Pearl Harbor in 1941.

State Capitol Building, Sacramento. (Copyright Christopher P. Baker)

California State Railroad Museum. (Copyright Christopher P. Baker)

California State Railroad Museum
1255 I Street • 916-445-5995
www.californiarailroad.museum

✓ You'll be wowed from start to finish as you step back in time at this world-class tribute to the role of the "iron horse" in California's history and evolution. Located in the Old Sacramento Waterfront District, this roundhouse museum displays 19 meticulously restored locomotives dating from 1862 to 1944, plus period-perfect walk-through railway cars from the golden age of railroads in the American West. The collection includes eight of the fewer than 45 full-size steam locomotives built prior to 1880 still extant in the United States. Fabulous full-scale dioramas include an 1860s railroad construction site high in the Sierra Nevada. Plus, a high-speed train simulator allows you to feel what it's like to pilot a modern high-speed locomotive.

Kids will especially appreciate **Small Wonders: The Magic of Toy Trains**, including some 1,000 toy trains and a fantastic operating layout. And if you're yearning for the old days, on spring and summer weekends (April–September), hop aboard the museum-operated **Sacramento Southern Railroad steam train**, which departs from the nearby Central Pacific Railroad Freight Depot for a scenic excursion.

Lemon Grass

601 Monroe Street • 916-486-4891
www.lemongrassrestaurant.com

✓ Chef-owner Mai Pham's awarding-winning Vietnamese/
Thai restaurant has been a local institution for three
decades and put Southeast Asia cuisine on the local map with
its authentic and dazzlingly flavorful dishes. Renovated a decade
ago to reflect Sacramento's increasingly chic sophistication, its
look is eternally fresh.

All the traditional Vietnamese and Thai dishes are there: from
spring rolls, Pad Thai, Thai seafood curry, and bright-yellow
chicken satay with its tasty peanut sauce to Saigon crêpe,
garlicky-sweet clay-pot catfish, and pan-seared lemongrass ahi
tuna. As you'd hope, the Vietnamese salad rolls are crammed
full of noodles and poached shrimp and served with the perfect
dosage of mint and fresh basil. The curries feature pink prawns,
perfectly done chunks of chicken, plus the freshest of veggies
and peppers swimming in fragrant curry coconut milk sauce.
Vegetarians will appreciate the broad selection, including to-
die-for crispy vegetable rolls, stuffed with wood ear mushrooms
and shredded taro and served with a soy-lime dipping sauce.
Desserts are no less enticing—from chunky ginger ice cream to
chocolate orange cake.

Lemon Grass.
(Courtesy
Lemon Grass)

Nearby Alternatives

Museum: Sutter's Fort State Historic Park and State Indian Museum

In 1841, Swiss immigrant John Sutter built a fortified agricultural trading post named New Helvetia (later to become Sacramento). Sutter's Fort has been reconstructed, with gunsmith, blacksmith, and weaving shops. To its north, the **State Indian Museum** has marvelous exhibits on the native people's cultures, from before the Spanish until today.

Sutter's Fort State Historic Park
2701 L Street • 916-445-4422
www.parks.ca.gov/?page_id=485
State Indian Museum
2618 K Street • 916-324-0971
www.parks.ca.gov/?page_id=486

Venue: Old Sacramento Waterfront District

Sacramento's historic waterfront was the site of California's first booming business district, thanks to the 1849 gold rush. Today, this National Historic Landmark District and State Historic Park covering eight square blocks is a living history museum where docents in period costumes give tours. Check out the *Delta King* stern-wheeler!

1124 2nd Street • 916-442-8575
www.oldsacramento.com

Museum: Crocker Art Museum

Established in 1885 as the first public art museum west of the Mississippi, the downtown Crocker is Sacramento's premier cultural institution. Browse galleries brimming with world-class and globe-spanning works of art.

216 O Street • 916-808-7000
www.crockerart.org

Drive: Sacramento Delta Drive

Follow the winding levees through the marshy Sacramento River delta for a sensational 60-mile drive from **Suisun City**. Take time to spot wildfowl and raptors at **Rush Ranch Open Space**, ride restored electric trains at the **Western Railway Museum**, and stroll the old Chinese community of **Locke** before returning to Sacramento.

California Delta Chambers & Visitors Bureau
169 West Brannan Island Road, Isleton • 916-777-4041
www.californiadelta.org

Trip Planning

Sacramento Convention & Visitors Bureau
1608 I Street
916-808-7777
www.visitsacramento.com

LAKE TAHOE

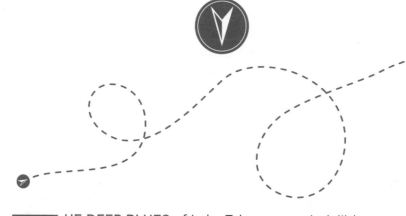

THE DEEP BLUES of Lake Tahoe are an indelible California icon. Studding the snowy, pine-clad Sierra Nevada mountains, the lake proves that a crown jewel is made complete by its setting. Picturesque is an understatement! The year-round destination is renowned in winter as California's premier ski resort and was good enough that the 1960 Winter Olympics were held here. In summer, Tahoe is a center for water-bound activities, while the snow-free slopes are nirvana for hiking, biking, and horseback treks.

Straddling the California-Nevada border, Lake Tahoe is two-faced (in the best sense of the word). Across the Nevada line, neon lights beckon with casinos, while California's lakeshore villages are replete with boutiques and great restaurants, from gourmet to rustic. Enjoy a cruise on a venerable stern-wheeler. Get high with a hot-air balloon ride. And don't fail to circumnavigate the lake on what many people hail as the most scenic drive in California.

Drive King's Beach to Emerald Bay

* West Shore Association • P.O. Box 844, Homewood
  www.westshorelaketahoe.com
* Sugar Point Pine State Park • State Park Road at Highway 89
  530-525-9528 • www.parks.ca.gov/?page_id=991

☑ Spend your morning driving the entire west side of Lake Tahoe. Begin at **King's Beach**, at the northern end of the lake, and head west on California 28 via the resorts of Carnelian Bay and Ridgewood to **Tahoe City**. Park at the North Tahoe Visitor Center, perfectly positioned for a walking tour, taking in the Lake Tahoe Dam and Gatekeeper's Museum. It showcases Tahoe history, from the Washoe people to the modern era of tourism. Also here, the **Museum of Sierra Ski History** regales the evolution of skiing, including mementos from the 1960 Winter Olympics.

Make **Eagle Rock** your next stop. A trail (between mile marker 67 and 68) leads up to this craggy volcanic outcrop offering a panoramic view of Lake Tahoe. Finally, stop at **Sugar Pine Point State Park** to roam the pine-shaded shoreline and explore the **Hellman Ehrman Mansion** (aka Pine Lodge). Listed on the National Register of Historic Places, this grandiose estate of 19th-century San Francisco banker Isaias W. Hellman sits on a knoll with a commanding view of Lake Tahoe.

Drive North Lake Tahoe to Emerald Bay. (Courtesy Lake Tahoe Visitors Authority)

Emerald Bay and *Dixie II*. (Credit Zephyr Cove Resort; courtesy Visit Lake Tahoe)

Emerald Bay State Park

Vikingsholm • 138 Emerald Bay Road • 530-541-6498
www.parks.ca.gov/?page_id=506

✔️ Emerald Bay is well-named. No other part of Lake Tahoe displays such unbelievably brilliant hues—emerald, turquoise, and jade of almost surreal perfection. The flask-shaped bay on Lake Tahoe's west shore is at the heart of 1,533-acre Emerald Bay State Park, a rugged wilderness region surrounding the bay. It's interspersed with hiking trails. So lace up and follow the **Eagle Falls Trail** for a great vantage point. With luck, you'll spot bald eagles!

Then head down the **Vikingsholm Trail** to the lakeshore for fabulous views of **Vikingsholm Castle**. This 38-room Scandinavian-style shoreline mansion built in 1929 is open for tours in summer. Feeling adventurous? Rent a kayak or stand-up paddleboard at Vikingsholm Beach or nearby **Baldwin Beach**, and paddle out to the bay's **Fannette Island**, topped by a now-derelict teahouse. You can even snorkel or (if suitably experienced and attired for cold water) scuba dive to explore the underwater **Emerald Bay Maritime Heritage Trail**, featuring four dive sites where several historic recreational boats, launches, and barges have been purposely sunk by the park service.

Tahoe House Bakery & Gourmet

625 West Lake Boulevard, Tahoe City
530-583-1377 • www.tahoe-house.com

✓ Locals swear by this cozy, family-owned Tahoe City bakery-restaurant and grocery, which has been making scrumptious goodies since 1977, when Swiss immigrants Peter and Helen Vogt set up shop to bake delicious European-style breads. They also bake incredible cakes, cookies, muffins, and pastries, from fruit tarts and cinnamon rolls to chocolate croissants . . . even bagels! And the still-warm apple strudel and ham-and-cheese croissants are to die for. Plus, with such yummy crusty breads, you can't go wrong with a freshly made gourmet sandwich, an Asian orzo salad, creamy dill cucumber salad, or another delish deli salad, which change daily. On cold days, you might prefer a homemade hot soup or a chicken potpie. You can enjoy eating by the fire in winter or out on a patio in summer.

A small gourmet grocery section sells Tahoe House's specialty sauces, marinades, and dressings, plus cheeses, cured meats, and more. And there's no better place for an organic coffee or espresso (or latte or mocha), with each fresh-ground cup made to order in their Swiss coffee maker.

Tahoe House Bakery & Gourmet. (Courtesy Tahoe House Bakery & Gourmet)

Nearby Alternatives

Activity: Cruise the Lake on the MS *Dixie II*

To admire the lake more closely, hop aboard the MS *Dixie II* stern-wheeler for a 2.5-hour cruise from Zephyr Cove Resort to Emerald Bay. You'll experience a new facet of the 13-mile-wide peacock-blue jewel while admiring the pristine alpine scenery—and sunset—from the outside decks on the narrated cruise.
Zephyr Cove Resort
760 US Hwy. 50, Zephyr Cove
775-589-4907
www.zephyrcove.com

Outdoors: Echo Summit and Echo Lake

Make the sensational scenic drive south up US Route 50 to Echo Summit for a staggering view. Then head to nearby Lower Echo Lake to swim, fish, and hike the five-mile out-and-back, dog-friendly lakeside trail. You can rent fishing boats and kayaks in summer.
Johnson Pass Road,
off US Route 50
www.tahoesouth.com/hike/
echo-lakes-trail

Venue: Truckee

Once a raucous 19th-century mining and railroad town, today Truckee's Old-West downtown is a bohemian hub perfect for exploring on foot. Check out its **Old Jail Museum**, historic **train depot**, and such art galleries as the **Mountain Arts Collective**. For an adrenaline rush, go whitewater rafting down the Truckee River.
Truckee Chamber of Commerce
10065 Donner Pass Road
530-587-2757
www.truckee.com

Outdoors: Donner Memorial State Park and Donner Summit

Named for the 81-member Donner Party that in November 1846 became trapped by snow and, according to legend, resorted to cannibalism, this mountain pass has spectacular vistas over Donner Lake. The latter has biking and hiking trails, rock climbing, beaches, and the superb **Emigrant Trail Museum** regaling local history.
12953 Donner Pass Road
530-582-7894
www.donnersummitca.com

Trip Planning

Lake Tahoe Visitors Authority
4114 Lake Tahoe Boulevard,
South Lake Tahoe • 530-542-4637
www.visitinglaketahoe.com
www.tahoesouth.com
Tahoe City Visitor Center
100 North Lane Boulevard,
Tahoe City • 530-581-6900
www.gotahoenorth.com

GOLD COUNTRY

THERE'S NO SHORTAGE of nuggets to be discovered along Highway 49, the "Mother Lode Highway" running north-south the 130-mile length of Gold Country. An ideal 24 hours would concentrate in either the northern or southern half or the central core (as here), focusing on each region's history-rich towns once at the center of the hard-rock mining fields.

History buffs are in heaven, and not simply because these towns resemble living history museums, with their quintessential Old West architecture. Pan for gold like a pioneer at the Marshall Gold Discovery State Historic Park, where James Marshall discovered gold in 1848. Hit the wineries of the Shenandoah Valley to sample the renowned AVA's best vintages. Explore the underground California Cavern, and giant redwood groves at Calaveras Big Trees State Park. Ride an old steam train at Jamestown's Railtown 1897 State Historic Park or even an old stagecoach at Columbia State Historic Park.

Marshall Gold Discovery State Park

310 Back Street, Coloma · 530-622-3470
www.parks.ca.gov/?page_id=484

☑ Don't miss one of the most significant historic sites in California! It was here in 1848, on the South Fork of the American River, that James W. Marshall discovered gold, sparking the gold rush. The tailrace of Sutter's original sawmill (in which Marshall spotted gold flakes) is still visible, although the sawmill itself is a reconstruction. You can even learn to pan for gold behind **Bekeart's Gun Shop**, then purchase a pan at the **Marshall Gold Mercantile**, and try your luck down by the river.

Begin at the visitor center and museum, where interpretive exhibits make the past come alive, including of the Native American cultures present before the gold rush, as well as the Chinese coolies imported to do much of the labor. Now you can explore the more than 20 historic buildings dispersed to both sides of the road amid the riparian oak woodlands. Finally, hike the Monument Trail uphill to the hilltop **Marshall Monument**, pointing down to the place of discovery and where Marshall is buried. Guided walking tours are offered.

Marshall Gold Discovery State Park, panning for gold. (Courtesy Visit Placer)

Columbia State Historic Park, stagecoach. (Courtesy Visit Tuolumne County)

Columbia State Historic Park

22708 Broadway Street, Columbia • 209-588-9128
www.parks.ca.gov/?page_id=552

✓ If there's one de rigueur visit in Gold Country, it's
Columbia—the former "Gem of the Southern Mines" and
the state's second-largest city at the peak of the gold rush.
Boasting the largest collection of gold rush–era structures in
California, Columbia State Historic Park is preserved as a living
museum dedicated to transporting visitors metaphorically back
in time to experience life in bustling gold rush California. It truly
does feel like stepping back two centuries, not least because
merchants and docents dress in 1850s attire. Plus, no cars are
allowed, though you'll definitely hear the clip-clop of horses!

Start with a ride through town on the stagecoach. Then admire
the blacksmith forging red-hot horseshoes on an anvil. Let the
kids pan for gold at the **Matelot Gulch Mining** store, quench your
thirst with a cold sarsaparilla soda in a Western-style saloon, and
dress up in yesteryear costumes for an old-time photo in the
portrait studio. For a fun-filled, in-depth understanding of life as
it was 150-plus years ago, take a guided tour with a docent.

Crusco's

1240 Main Street, Angel Camp • 209-736-1440
www.facebook.com/Cruscos

✓ Angel Camp's iconic and homey Crusco's Ristorante Italiano has been drawing a fiercely loyal clientele for its authentically Italian dishes for more than two decades. It's housed in an appropriately Mediterranean-looking, weathered 150-year-old building with exposed brownstone walls looking like a piece of Tuscany transplanted. Traditional Italian music adds to the class-act charm.

The kitchen puts out a genuine northern Italian menu, frequently updated following the owners' regular research trips to Italy. Simply reading your menu options may cause you to salivate. Perhaps you'll choose the Polenta Antonella dish (creamy cornmeal with chicken and mushroom sauce); gnocchi with wild fire Gorgonzola cheese, Asian pear, and pine nuts; or a pork osso bucco with creamy polenta. The focaccia is made in-house, as are all the pastas and the hot calabrese-style Italian sausage. Look for the nightly specials, paired with Italian or local award-winning wines. The lunch menu is more varied and includes sandwiches, burgers, and salads. And the menu includes gluten-free and vegetarian options, as well as such divine homemade desserts as *panna cotta* or chocolate truffle torte.

Crusco's Ristorante ravioli. (Courtesy Crusco's Ristorante)

Nearby Alternatives

Venue: Auburn

Auburn—once site of the richest goldfield of all—continued to thrive after the gold ran out, and today it's the largest town in Gold Country. Pick up a Self-Guided Historical Walking Tour brochure at the California Welcome Center, and then spend a half-day discovering this California Historical Landmark's 46 sites.
California Welcome Center
1103 High Street
530-887-2111
www.visitplacer.com

Outdoors: Calaveras Big Trees State Park

You don't need to be a nature lover to feel humbled hiking among the biggest trees on earth. The park, high above Angels Camp, preserves two groves of giant sequoias. The North Grove has the biggest trees; the less-visited and more remote South Grove is quieter and has longer trails.
1170 East Highway 4, Arnold
209-795-3840
www.parks.ca.gov/?page_id=551

Venue: Sutter Creek and Shenandoah Valley

The prettiest of mining-era towns is nicknamed the "Jewel of the Gold Country." Don't miss Knight Foundry (*www.knightfoundry.com*), a wizards' workshop that is America's last water-powered foundry and machine shop; and the Kennedy Gold Mine (*www.kennedygoldmine.com*). Nearby, the warm Shenandoah Valley is famous for zinfandel wineries (*www.amadorwine.com*).
Sutter Creek Visitors Center
71A Main Street
209-267-5647, ext. 302
www.suttercreek.org

Venue: Railtown 1897 State Historic Park

Ride a historic steam train (weekends, April–October) through scenic Gold Country as the highlight of a visit to this 19th-century railroad depot in Jamestown. Still functioning as a locomotive maintenance facility, it has a working roundhouse, belt-driven machine and blacksmithing shop, and an excellent interpretive center.
10501 Reservoir Road, Jamestown
209-984-3953
www.railtown1897.org

Trip Planning

Gold Country Visitors Association
1201 CA-49, Angels Camp
800-225-3764
www.visitgoldcountry.com

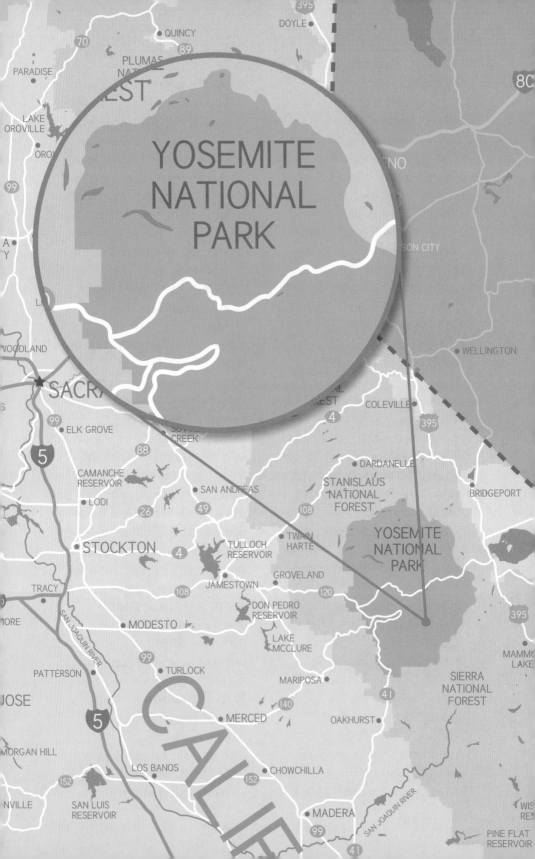

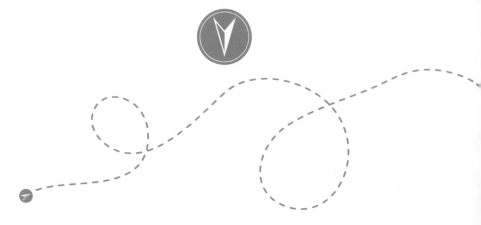

YOSEMITE NATIONAL PARK

AS THE MOST celebrated national park in California, Yosemite is indisputably North America's most superlative expression of natural grandeur. Most famous for its huge valley with sheer rock walls from which waterfalls cascade thousands of feet, the park encompasses a vast expanse of High Sierra spanning alpine meadows, sequoia redwood forests, and bare granitic landscapes of unsurpassed beauty. No wonder this dramatic venue teems with visitors in summer, at least in the glacier-carved valley—the heart of the park.

The valley represents only one percent of the park. With so many other beauty spots, it's easy to escape the madding crowds, not least by visiting in winter, when a blanket of snow adds to the staggering beauty. Spring (when the wildflowers are in bloom) and autumn are especially good times for spotting wildlife, perhaps even black bears! Be sure to check the National Park website, loaded with useful maps and practical information.

Valley Loop Trail

Yosemite Valley Visitor Center • 9035 Village Drive • 209-372-2000
www.nps.gov/yose/planyourvisit/valleylooptrail.htm

☑ There's no better way to spend the morning than hiking the eastern half of the flat Valley Loop Trail. You'll get a grand perspective of almost all the iconic, jaw-dropping features as you loop seven miles through the valley. Take the free Valley Visitor Shuttle to **Lower Yosemite Fall** (shuttle stop #6), and follow the gentle slope to the base of the 2,495-foot cascade. Below, the view from **Cooks Meadow** offers a grand panorama, including Half Dome, El Capitan, and Sentinel Falls. Westward, the well-groomed trail follows the Merced River through meadows at the base of granite cliffs to **El Capitan**.

After spotting the climbers from **El Capitan Meadow**, cross the river on El Capitan Bridge and return to Yosemite Village via **Sentinel Beach**. Further along is the quaint **Yosemite Chapel**, dating from 1878 and set amid a copse that provides a stupendous photo-op in autumn, with Half Dome behind as a backdrop. Shortly beyond, cross the Merced River along Sentinel Drive and make your way to **The Awahnee**, the crown jewel of Yosemite hotels.

Yosemite Falls from Cooks Meadow. (Copyright Christopher P. Baker)

Half Dome and Vernal Falls from Glacier Point. (Copyright Christopher P. Baker)

Drive to Glacier Park

Glacier Point Road · 209-372-2000
www.nps.gov/yose/planyourvisit/glacierpoint.htm

☑ Glacier Point, at an elevation of 7,214 feet, overlooks Yosemite Village 3,214 feet below. Standing at the viewpoint edge is unnerving, as the vertical rock wall is twice as high (and just as sheer) as the Empire State Building! The 32-mile drive—exit the valley on Wawona Road (SR 41)—will take at least one hour each way, with added time to photograph the valley from **Tunnel View**: the classic view that Ansel Adams made famous.

Eight miles further south, turn left and follow Glacier Point Road (open May to November, depending on snowfall) as it snakes steadily uphill to the viewpoint, accessed via a wheelchair-friendly trail from the parking lot. You can stand transfixed for hours as you admire the panoramic view of Half Dome, Vernal Falls, Yosemite Falls, Yosemite Village (far, far below), and the crest of the Sierra Nevada Mountains. Linger for the sunset, when the setting sun gilds Half Dome in gold.

A shuttle tour bus departs Yosemite Lodge daily at 8:30 a.m. and 1:30 p.m. You can book one way, and hike back down to the valley—a tough descent (take the morning shuttle)!

The Awahnee Dining Room

The Awahnee Hotel • 1 Awahnee Drive • 209-372-1489
www.travelyosemite.com/dining/the-ahwahnee-dining-room

✔ Because the historic eponymous hotel is a destination in its own right, it's no surprise that its restaurant is an immensely popular "destination dining spot." The Awahnee Hotel was built of granite and timbers in 1927 as The Majestic Yosemite Hotel. With towering 34-foot-high ceilings, granite pillars supporting enormous pine trestles, and floor-to-ceiling windows, the Gothic chandelier-lit dining room is a spectacular venue for breakfast, lunch, dinner, or its legendary Sunday "Grand Brunch," offering everything from omelets to oysters. Open year-round, this opulent dining room is the setting for the world-renowned Bracebridge Dinner (lucky patrons are chosen by lottery).

The seasonal menu always includes rotisserie-cooked chicken, succulent steaks, and seafood, plus the restaurant's signature boysenberry pie—a staple for half a century. Casual dress is permitted at breakfast, brunch, and lunch. But note the dinner dress code restrictions: long pants and a collared shirt are required for men, while women must "wear a dress, skirt, or long pants with a blouse." Even children are "asked to dress for the occasion as well." Reservations are strongly advised.

The Ahwahnee Hotel. (Copyright Amadscientist, CC BY-SA 3.0, via Wikimedia Commons)

Nearby Alternatives

Outdoors: Hike Vernal Falls

Allow three hours to hike the strenuous 2.5-mile trail to the top of Vernal Falls via the **John Muir Trail**, which begins at shuttle shop #16 in the valley. Diverting onto the **Mist Trail**, the switchback "giant staircase" grants spectacular, up-close views, with spray splashing your every step to the top of the cascade.
www.nps.gov/
yose/planyourvisit/
vernalnevadatrail.htm

Outdoors: Mariposa Grove of Big Trees

Hike (or, in winter, snowshoe) the largest sequoia grove in Yosemite to be awestruck by its more than 500 mature giant sequoias. The moderate two-mile **Grizzly Giant Loop Trail** leads to the 3,000-year-old **Grizzly Giant** and **California Tunnel Tree**. The seven-mile **Mariposa Grove Trail** offers a real workout to distant upper groves.
Mariposa Grove Road
209-372-0200
www.nps.gov/yose/
planyourvisit/mg.htm

Activity: Tubing on the Merced River

Conditions permitting in summer, rent a raft in Yosemite or plop your own inner tube into the Merced River, and spend the afternoon drifting downstream. Put in at Stoneman Bridge, and take out at Sentinel Beach Picnic Area (a lazy three-mile journey), with time for swimming in the cool water.
Curry Village Tour & Activities Kiosk
Curry Village Drive
888-413-8869
www.travelyosemite.com/ things-to-do/rafting
www.nps.gov/yose/ planyourvisit/water.htm

Outdoors: Tuolumne Meadows

Accessed from the valley via Tioga Pass Road (SR 120), this large high-elevation alpine meadow at 8,600 feet is a glorious place to soak in the alpine tranquility. The dramatic drive from the valley includes such de rigueur scenic stops as **Olmsted Point** and **Tenaya Lake**, and beyond the meadow, the plunging **Tioga Pass** descent to Mono Lake.
www.nps.gov/yose/
planyourvisit/tm.htm
w ww.nps.gov/yose/learn/
nature/tuolumne.htm

Trip Planning

Yosemite National Park
9035 Village Drive
209-372-0200
www.nps.gov/yose

MENDOCINO

SURELY ONE OF the top 10 destinations of California, this perfectly manicured and #instaready coastal hamlet boasts a dramatic ocean-bluff setting, a thriving artistic community, and a choice of romantic gingerbread B&Bs and quaint restaurants. Mendocino is so charming and walkable, it's hard to imagine that it began as a raucous mid-19th-century logging port.

You'll be blown away by the breathtaking coastal scenery, which is reason enough to visit. The most scenic swathes are protected in a string of state parks that also preserve precious redwood groves and pygmy forest: Van Damme State Park is the closest to Mendocino. Hike or bicycle the trails. Hop aboard the Skunk Train for a ride into the redwoods on a centenary puffing billy. Slip into a kayak or outrigger canoe to paddle Mendocino Bay or Big Bend River. Fort Ross State Historic Park and Point Arena Lighthouse are among the fascinating historic sights close by.

Walking Tour

Kelley House Museum • 45007 Albion Street
707-937-5791 • www.kelleyhousemuseum.org

✓ California's only coastal town designated as a Historic
Preservation District is understandable: the quaint town is
all cute 19th-century gingerbread New England–style mansions
and cottages. Just six blocks wide by 10 short blocks long,
Mendocino's Lilliputian-scale begs you to park your car and
stroll. Your best option is to join a delightfully informative guided
tour offered by the **Kelley House Museum** given by docents
wearing period costumes.

If you prefer to go it alone, start at the museum, which does
a great job profiling local history. Now walk west along bayfront
Main Street to the **Mendocino Hotel**, an 1878 structure with a
quintessential faux-Western façade. Turn right to Albion, and
walk east past the quaint **MacCallum House**. Turn left on Lansing
Street to admire the former **Masonic Lodge** topped by a carved
statue of Father Time and a maiden. At Little Lake Street, turn
left, then turn right on Kasten Street for the **Mendocino Arts
Center** to browse its galleries and store. Finally, stroll west
along Little Lake Street to **Mendocino Headlands**, with its surf-
pounded promontory.

Mendocino village. (Courtesy Visit Mendocino)

Van Damme State Park. (Courtesy Visit Mendocino)

Van Damme State Park

8125 North Highway 1, Little River • 707-937-5804
www.parks.ca.gov/?page_id=433

✓ Three miles south of Mendocino, this state park recedes
inland from a half-moon cove and extends uphill through
the lush fern-filled canyon of the Little River to a pygmy forest
of stunted, wind-bowed cypress and pine trees. Laced by 10
miles of trails, plus a paved road perfect for cyclists, it's a popular
wilderness escape for hiking, which is made more so by having a
protected beach and sea caves for exploring. Guided kayak tours
are offered from the parking lot in summer. You can even dive
here if you bring your own gear.

Start at the **Van Damme Visitor Center**, notable for its diorama
of an underwater surge channel complete with all the critters
that inhabit the tidal environment. Then hike the Fern Canyon
Scenic Trail and Pygmy Forest loop: in all, an eight-mile round-
trip hike (depending on which route you choose). For a shorter
walk, drive along Airport Road to the (signed) Pygmy Forest
Trail—a four-mile loop that includes Fern Canyon and redwood
forest. Keep your ears and eyes open for pileated woodpeckers.

McCallum House

45020 Albion Street, Mendocino • 707-937-0289 • www.maccallumhouse.com

✓ One look at this romantic white gingerbread manse dating from 1882, and you immediately sense the possibilities of a culinary treat. In fact, this superb boutique B&B restaurant is acclaimed as the area's best. The casually elegant restaurant occupies the former library, graced by wood paneling, two river stone fireplaces, and fresh-cut flowers on every table.

Chef Alan Kantor was a pioneer in sustainable dining, using only the highest-quality and freshest organic products from local farms and fisheries. The seasonal menu showcases imaginative California nouvelle dishes guaranteed to wow your taste buds. Appetizers of pan-seared scallops or chive potato gnocchi gratin with mushrooms, prosciutto, and Sonoma dry jack cheese are on the menu, and you can't go wrong with the ahi poke bowl, or the Grilled Niman Ranch Steak served with grilled asparagus, crispy fingerlings, and bourbon butter sauce. Meal portions are generous. Still, treat yourself to poppyseed beignets with Chantilly cream, or a chocolate fudge brownie dessert with chocolate cherry ice cream. Divine! Now retire to the veranda with a cocktail to watch the sun go down.

MacCallum House, oyster taco. (Credit J. Perlman; courtesy McCallum House)

Nearby Alternatives

Activity: Paddle Big Bend River

For a change of pace and scenery, paddle the Big Bend Estuary, which opens into Mendocino Bay. Catch A Canoe, at the mouth of the river, rents Polynesian-style redwood outrigger canoes and polyethylene kayaks for two-hour solo and guided trips. Keep your eyes peeled for harbor seals and river otters.

**Catch A Canoe
1 South Big River Road, Mendocino
707-937-0273
www.catchacanoe.com**

Activity: Skunk Train

Who wouldn't thrill to a ride on an old steam train through the redwood forest? You'll chug past Pudding Creek Estuary and up into the Coast Range foothills on the 90-minute round-trip ride, hauled by a Baldwin 2-8-2 Mikado locomotive. Alternatively, you can pedal yourself on an electric-powered rail-bike!

**100 West Laurel Street, Fort Bragg
707-964-6371
www.skunktrain.com**

Venue: Point Arena Lighthouse

Isolated Point Arena is pinned by a 115-foot-tall lighthouse built in 1908 and originally powered by a Fresnel lens. Today, the beacon is an LED array, but you can view the original 258-prism lens in the museum, and then climb the spiral tower staircase for a panoramic view along this wild coast.

**45500 Lighthouse Road, Point Arena
707-882-2809, ext. 1
www.pointarenalighthouse.com**

Venue: Fort Ross State Historic Park

Once a thriving tsarist Russian settlement (1812–1842), this site retains its wooden stockade and original structures, plus a reconstructed Russian Orthodox chapel, barracks, and even the windmill. The visitor center has superb interpretive exhibits, including of the Kashia Pomo peoples resident before the Russian arrival and the subsequent ranching era.

**19005 Coast Highway 1
707-847-3286
www.parks.ca.gov/?page_id=449**

Trip Planning

Visit Mendocino County

**105 West Clay Street, Ukiah
707-964-9010
www.visitmendocino.com**

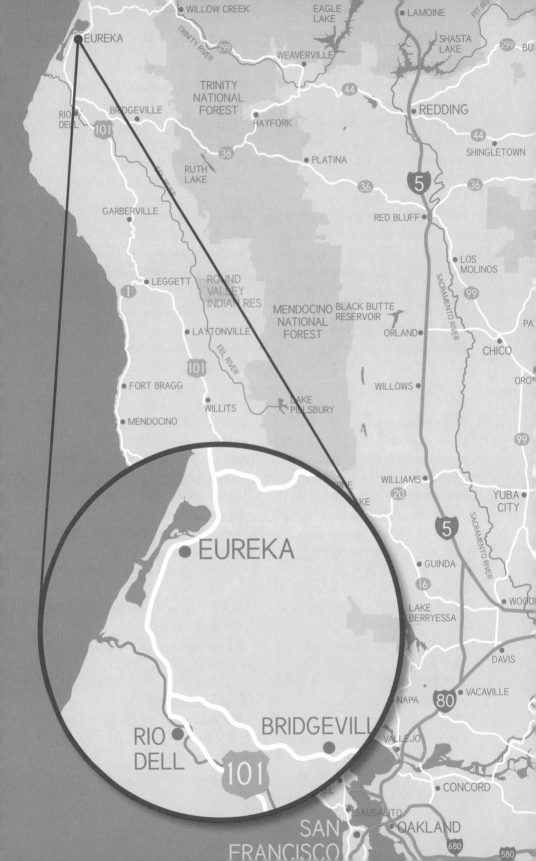

EUREKA

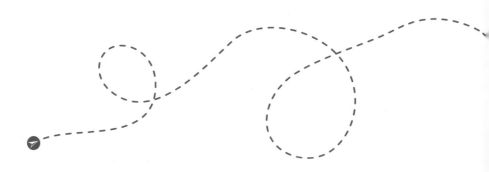

THE LARGEST COASTAL city between San Francisco and Portland has a charming split personality. Rusty fishing boats straight out of *Forrest Gump* still fill the harbor. Logging trucks still rumble through town. And the entire Victorian-era Old Town district is a trove of ornate 19th-century homes that reach their zenith with the Queen Anne Carson Mansion. Eureka's yesteryear ambience makes a fitting venue for the must-see Blue Ox Millworks Historic Park, which keeps alive traditional Victorian-era crafts from blacksmithing to woodworking.

The town is surrounded by nature at its finest. Above all, of course, there are miles and miles of pristine coast redwood forests just waiting for you to explore, most magnificently along the "Avenue of the Giants." Then there's the "Lost Coast"—truly a lonesome Shangri-la accessed via mountainous Humboldt Redwood State Park from either of the two small old-world towns of Ferndale and Garberville, which are destinations in their own right.

Old Town Eureka

* Eureka Visitor Center/Clark Historical Museum • 240 E Street
  707-443-1947 • www.clarkemuseum.org
* Humboldt Bay Tourism Center • 205 G Street
  707-672-3850 • www.visitredwoods.com

☑ Listed on the US National Register of Historic Places, magnificently preserved Old Town Eureka (founded in 1850 on the edge of Humboldt Bay) boasts more than 100 Victorian buildings. The greatest concentration of architecturally significant buildings is along E, F, and G Streets, and First, Second, and Third Streets. Walk these six blocks and let serendipity be your guide. You'll be astounded by the eclectic architecture along the way, including Greek Revival, Italianate, Eastlake, and Queen Anne. Art lovers should call in at the excellent **Morris Graves Museum of Art** (*636 F Street, www. humboldtarts.org*) in the Eureka Carnegie Library. And history buffs can catch up on local history at the **Clarke Historical Museum** (*240 E Street, www.clarkemuseum.org*) in the landmark neoclassical Bank of Eureka Building.

Eureka's pride and joy is the astonishing **Carson Mansion** (*M Street and 2nd Street*). Built in 1884 as the home of lumber baron, William Carson, it's one of America's finest examples of Queen Anne architecture and perhaps its most extravagant! Now a private club, it's not open to the public.

Old Town Eureka. (Courtesy Eddy Communications)

Avenue of the Giants. (Courtesy Visit Redwoods)

Avenue of the Giants

Humboldt Redwoods Visitor Center • 17119 Avenue of the Giants, Weott
707-946-2263 • www.visitredwoods.com • www.avenueofthegiants.net

☑ Acclaimed as the finest forest drive in the world, the 31-mile portion of State Route 254 known as the "Avenue of the Giants" is truly a sublime experience. Redwood National and State Parks, *north* of Eureka, have taller trees, but Humboldt Redwood State Park's Avenue of the Giants, south of Eureka, offers by far the most impressive display of these enormous trees in the entire 500-mile coast redwood belt. The scenic route begins just south of Scotia, ends just north of Garberville, and parallels Highway 101 and the South Fork of the Eel River.

Take your time! Stop to photograph, hike, and maybe cool your heels in the Eel River—a federally designated Wild & Scenic Waterway with idyllic bathing and fishing spots. Several trailheads along the route offer a chance to park and stroll away from the traffic to savor the pristine silence of the largest remaining stand of virgin redwoods in the world. The Founders Grove Trail leads to the **Dyerville Giant**, the park's tallest tree (362 feet) until it fell over in 1991.

Restaurant 301

301 L Street • 707-444-8062 • www.carterhouse.com/restaurant-301

☑ Oenophiles have a special reason to make a beeline to Restaurant 301 at Carter House Inn. The owners are wine connoisseurs and take their wine menu seriously. With an impressive list boasting more than 3,500 selections, plus wine and food pairings each evening, you're guaranteed to find the perfect bottle to go with your meal. Carter Cellars even makes its own award-winning wine!

The Chef's Grand Menu wine-paired tasting experiences are the house specialty and, along with the restaurant's season-driven, garden-to-table à la carte menu, change with the greens, vegetables, and herbs in the inn's on-site garden, plus such fresh regional ingredients as abalone, Dungeness crab, and scallops. In fact, Dungeness Crab Cakes are a house specialty, as are Humboldt beef tenderloin dishes with tangy out-of-this-world sauces that use cream, sherry, or just the right hint of wine. The kitchen also puts out its own beautifully marbleized breads. The bar serves locally brewed beers on tap plus classic cocktails. It's no wonder Restaurant 301 is considered among Northern California's best restaurants for a gastronomic adventure!

Restaurant 301 gnocchi.
(Courtesy Carter House)

Nearby Alternatives

Venue: Blue Ox Millworks Historic Park

A rarity in the modern high-tech world, this living history park is a fully functioning commercial sawmill and Victorian job shop that exists to preserve expert craftsmanship. You'll marvel at its custom woodworking, blacksmith shop, antique print shop, and ceramics studio, all entirely using 19th-century machinery.
One X Street • 707-444-3437
www.blueoxmill.com

Venue: Garberville

With its hippy culture and reputation for eccentricity, it's impossible not to love this quirky heart-of-the-redwoods former lumbering town. You can even hunt for Bigfoot, the mythical creature that frequents surrounding forests. Plus, it's the southern gateway to the Avenue of the Giants.
Southern Humboldt Chamber of Commerce
782 Redwood Drive
707-923-2613
www.garberville.org

Venue: Ferndale

Hollywood loves Ferndale for its ornate and exquisitely preserved Victorian homes, and so will you! Nestled between Eureka, the redwoods, and the fabled Lost Coast, this small town—on the National Register of Historic Places in entirety—encapsulates old-fashioned Americana. Its enchanting "Butterfat Palaces" today house art galleries, boutiques, and the **Ferndale Museum** (*www.ferndalemuseum.com*).
Ferndale Chamber of Commerce
580 Main Street
707-796-4477
www.visitferndale.com

Outdoors: Lost Coast

It's California's only coastal wilderness without road access. But north of Punta Gorda, you *can* drive a scenic route over the mountains and along the shore between Ferndale and exit 663 off US 101. The snaking route leads through Humboldt Redwoods State Park and the hamlet of Petrolia. Experienced hikers can tackle the 25-mile-long **Lost Coast Trail** between Punta Gorda Lighthouse and Shelter Cove.
www.visitredwoods.com/listing/lost-coast-scenic-drive/148

Trip Planning

Visitor Center

201 E Street • 707-798-6411
www.visiteureka.com

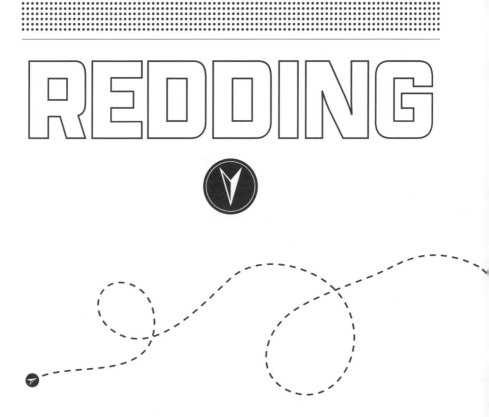

REDDING

GATEWAY TO NORTHERN California's outdoor paradise, Redding is easily the region's "first" city, and it's perfectly positioned for hub-and-spoke exploring of the area's stupendous top draws. Most famously, to the north, is iconic snowcapped Mt. Shasta; to the east lies Lassen Volcano National Park, with its bubbling mud pools and lakes. Each is deserving of a full day and can hardly be done in less. But Redding itself is a lovely city, renowned for its Sundial Bridge and the adjoining—and excellent—Turtle Bay Exploration Park and Museum. And just north of town, Shasta Dam and Shasta Lake are prime destinations.

Above all, Redding is a base for outdoor enthusiasts, including fishers keen to cast for wild trout and salmon. Lake Shasta Caverns is a popular place to cool off in hot summer months. The area abounds in #instaready waterfalls, such as around Dunsmuir. And Castle Crags State Park combines great hiking with geological marvels.

Walking Tour

Redding Convention & Visitors Bureau Visitor Center • 1448 Pine Street
530-225-4100 • www.visitredding.com

☑ With so much natural beauty for miles around, it would be easy to skip through Redding without realizing what you're missing. But invest half a day to explore the city's concentrated prime attractions, such as the historic **Cascade Theatre**. Its signature site is the "bird in flight"-design **Sundial Bridge**. The 710-foot-wide, cantilevered, pedestrian suspension bridge spanning the Sacramento River is an eye-pleasing marvel. It's also the world's largest sundial. You'll walk atop translucent glass, illuminated from beneath at night.

The bridge extends across the river from the **Turtle Bay Exploration Park and Museum** on its south side. Begin at this 300-acre campus, with its magnificent interactive exhibits that explore the relationship between humans and nature—from Native American history to a huge butterfly house, plus an underground aquarium focused on the life of salmon, for which the river is famous. Across the bridge awaits the **McConnell Arboretum and Gardens**, cleverly designed to meld into the natural environment. Plus, the Sacramento River Trail leads the **River Aquatic Center**—a perfect place to cool off on hot days.

Redding walking tour, Sundial Bridge. (Courtesy Visit Redding)

Mount Shasta, tundra swans. (Copyright USFWS; courtesy Wikipedia)

Mt. Shasta

Mt. Shasta Chamber of Commerce & Visitor Center • 300 Pine Street
530-926-4865 • www.visitmtshasta.com

✔ Mt. Shasta's famously snowcapped Fuji-esque peak soars to 14,179 feet in elevation, its beauty so intoxicating that naturalist John Muir's "blood turned to wine" on first sight in 1874. The classic cone-shaped volcano is a year-round destination for outdoorsy types. First stop, though, is the gateway **town of Mt. Shasta**, described by the California Tourism Board as a "New Agey enclave," and a perfect base for exploring the massive stratovolcano topped by glaciers. Lake Street runs north from town as the Everitt Memorial Highway, taking you to the timberline at around 8,000 feet.

In late spring and summer, hiking gets no better than amid the mountain's wildflower-strewn meadows dotted throughout Shasta-Trinity National Forest (*www.fs.usda.gov*), and it's good for spotting eagles, deer, and maybe even black bears. Climbers can summit the mountain (a guide is recommended). There's even world-class fishing. And you can rent mountain bikes in town to hit the mountain trails. Needless to say, in winter, downhill skiers flock to **Mt. Shasta Ski Park** (*www.skipark.com*), while the slopes are also nirvana for sledding, snowshoeing, and cross-country skiing.

C.R. Gibbs American Grill

230 Hilltop Drive, Redding • 530-221-2335 • www.crgibbs.com

☑ This award-winning and iconic downtown Redding restaurant has been serving fine food for three generations and almost half a century. Attached to the Best Western Plus hotel, its casual atmosphere appeals to an eclectic potpourri of patrons. But C.R. Gibbs is far more than a mere "chain hotel" diner serving American grill-style cuisine. The open kitchen delivers filling and satisfaction-inducing classic Californian dishes using fresh, seasonal ingredients.

Although the hearty breakfast menu doesn't change (think pancakes or sweet French toast, and veggie-rich scrambles), the eclectic lunch and dinner menus reflect whatever goodies are in season locally. Salads and sandwiches include a delicious Firecracker Prawn Salad; "Ancho Chicken," southern fried with ancho chili honey, pepper jack cheese, and Cajun aioli; and a California club wrap. The crew also fires up traditional brick-oven pizzas and sizzles a large range of burgers. Rib eye steak? No problem! Or maybe you'd prefer the lighter Shrimp Bowl, a meant-to-be-shared family platter; Olde English Fish 'n' Chips; or, in season, a fresh-grilled salmon special with mussels atop pasta. Enjoy!

C.R. Gibbs American Grill. (Courtesy Visit Redding)

Nearby Alternatives

Outdoors: Castle Crags State Park

In a region chock-full of geological superlatives, this state park is a standout. It's named for the massive glacier-polished spires and crags rising over the backcountry. Lace up your boots to explore miles of trails, from easy to the demanding 6.5-mile **Castle Dome Trail**, offering stupendous views of Mt. Shasta.
Castle Crags Road, Castella
530-235-2684
www.parks.ca.gov/?page_id=454

Outdoors: Shasta Dam and Shasta Lake

At 602 feet high, Shasta Dam was dwarfed only by the Hoover Dam and Grand Coulee Dam when completed in 1945. It's equally breathtaking for its majestic mountain-framed setting. Take a fascinating two-hour guided tour (free) of the powerhouse and other innards, and then relax on the lawns or cycle or hike the lakeside trails.
16349 Shasta Dam Boulevard, Shasta Lake
530-247-8555 (tours)
www.usbr.gov/mp/ncao

Outdoors: Lassen Volcanic National Park

You'd be driving far faster than speed limits permit to "do" Lassen Volcanic National Park in half a day. Plan the entire day to drive a circuit of this hissing, boiling volcanic wonderland surrounding by the snowcapped cone of Lassen Volcano. Hike the gentle **Bumpass Hell Trail** for fabulous views.
Kohm Yah-mah-nee Visitor Center
21820 Lassen National Park Highway
530-595-4480
www.nps.gov/lavo

Venue: Dunsmuir

Sprawling along the Sacramento River Valley between Redding and Shasta, pretty Dunsmuir, with its authentic 1920s look and feel, has two attractions of note: **Dunsmuir Botanical Garden** encompassing 10 acres nearby of delightful gardens, and trails that lead to the photogenic **Hedge Creek and Mossbrae waterfalls**.
Dunsmuir Chamber of Commerce & Visitor Center
5915 Dunsmuir Avenue
530-235-2177
www.dunsmuir.com

Trip Planning

Redding Convention and Visitors Bureau
1448 Pine Street
530-225-4100
www.visitredding.com

Index

Avenue of the Giants,
Chandelier Tree.
(Courtesy Visit Redwoods)